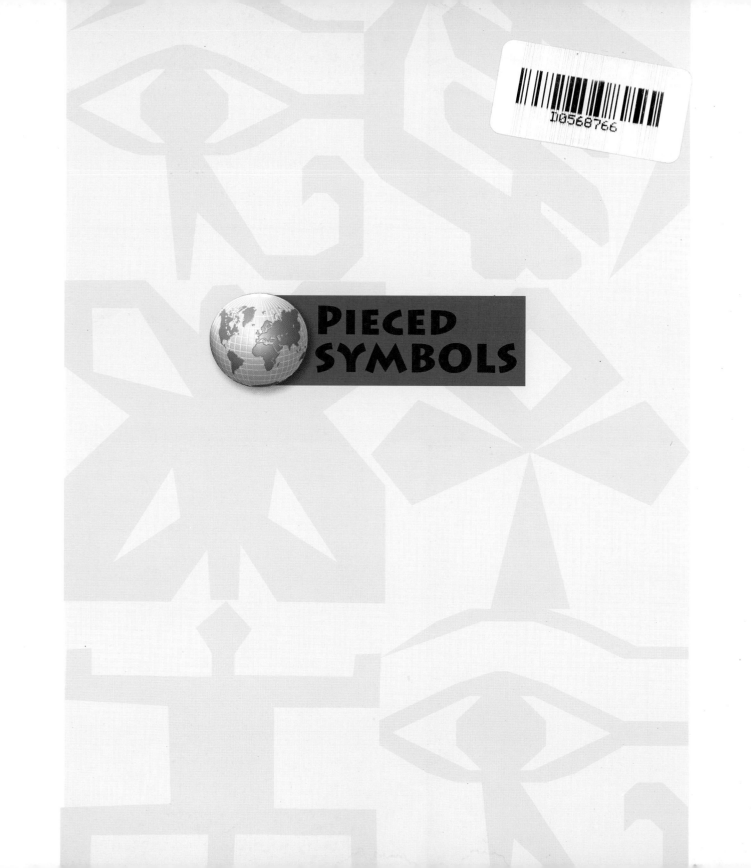

PIECED SYMBOLS

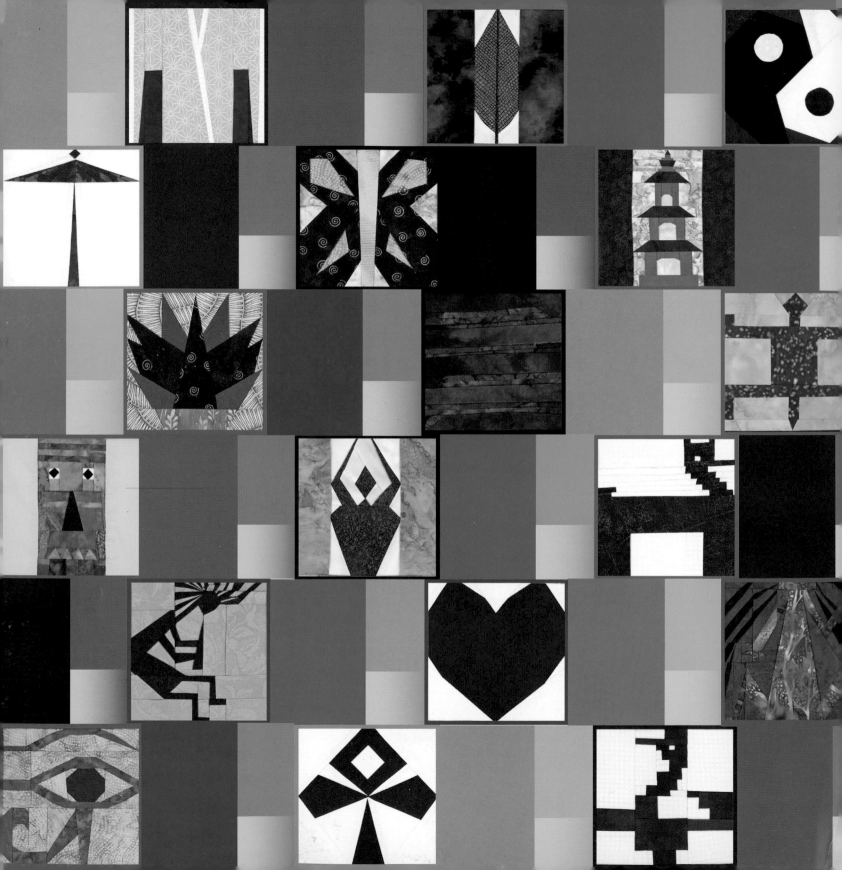

Pieced Symbols

Quilt Blocks from the Global Village

Myrah Brown Green

LARK BOOKS

A Division of Sterling Publishing Co., Inc.
New York / London

A Red Lips 4 Courage Communications, Inc. book
www.redlips4courage.com

Eileen Cannon Paulin
President

Catherine Risling
Director of Editorial

Senior Editor: Catherine Risling
Copy Editor: Ashlea Scaglione
Art Director: Susan H. Hartman
Illustrators: Edgar Barrientos and Jocelyn Foye
Production Designer: Jocelyn Foye
Photographer: Gregory Case

Library of Congress Cataloging-in-Publication Data

Green, Myrah Brown.
  Pieced symbols : quilt blocks from the global village /
Myrah Brown Green. -- 1st ed.
      p. cm.
  Includes index.
  ISBN 978-1-60059-424-3 (hc-plc with jacket : alk. paper)
  1. Quilting--Patterns. 2. Patchwork--Patterns. I. Title.
  TT835.G737 2009
  746.46'041--dc22

                          2008033525

10 9 8 7 6 5 4 3 2 1

First Edition

Published by Lark Books, A Division of
Sterling Publishing Co., Inc.
387 Park Avenue South, New York, NY 10016

Text © 2009, Myrah Brown Green
Photography © 2009, Red Lips 4 Courage Communications, Inc.
Illustrations © 2009, Red Lips 4 Courage Communications, Inc.

Distributed in Canada by Sterling Publishing,
c/o Canadian Manda Group, 165 Dufferin St.
Toronto, Ontario, Canada M6K 3H6

Distributed in the United Kingdom by GMC Distribution Services,
Castle Place, 166 High St., Lewes, East Sussex, England BN7 1XU

Distributed in Australia by Capricorn Link (Australia) Pty Ltd.,
P.O. Box 704, Windsor, NSW 2756 Australia

If you have questions or comments about this book, please contact:
Lark Books
67 Broadway
Asheville, NC 28801
(828) 253-0467

Manufactured in China

For information about custom editions, special sales, premium and
corporate purchases, please contact Sterling Special Sales Department
at (800) 805-5489 or specialsales@sterlingpub.com.

Contents

Foreword

Paulette Young
Cultural Anthropologist and
Independent Scholar, New York City

I became familiar with Myrah's passion for the arts of the African Diaspora while participating with her in an African textile and African American quilt exhibition at the Nathan Cummings Foundation in New York City in February 2008. During my initial encounter with Myrah, I was impressed with her vast knowledge of the arts of Africa and the Diaspora, and her keen artistic ability to incorporate various symbolic cultural forms in her quilts. The exhibition of Myrah's work evoked the presence of not only a master craftsperson, but also a gifted artist who transcended the medium. Her use of African and other non-Western symbols and her brilliant juxtaposition of color and shape expressed one inescapable fact: Myrah is an artist of profound talent.

Myrah's technical skills are enhanced by a powerful and exquisite sensibility. Her work flows out of life experiences garnered during a creative childhood spent in a multigenerational New England household in a culturally diverse neighborhood, as well as her knowledge of the varied achievements of traditional female textile artists in important textile centers throughout history.

Women across the globe have historically incorporated their lived experiences in a variety of artistic forms including textiles. Symbols are strongly influenced by oral tradition; women entrust these symbols with the responsibility for carrying certain messages that they may not entrust solely to language. Cloth's flat surface allows symbols to be displayed; the material is easily malleable to be wrapped around the body, styled into dress, or displayed to reflect the identity and values, not only of the creator, but also that of the owner.

Many of these production traditions inherited from the past and artistic techniques are present in Myrah's quilts. In this way, the experiences from the past combine with circumstances of the present to give meaning to her quilts. By selecting certain symbols in her cloth creations, Myrah incorporates ideas from her doctoral thesis, which focused on the presence of African symbols in Modern Art.

In *Pieced Symbols: Quilt Blocks from the Global Village*, Myrah explores and analyzes the meanings behind select cultural symbols. The principal contribution of this book is that it shows quilters how to incorporate the symbols from Africa, the Americas, Asia, Australia, and Europe in their quilt creations. Through her beautifully illustrated patterns, Myrah highlights the diverse cultural influences on her work. To the casual observer, Myrah's block designs appear as dynamic, colorful American textiles of high aesthetic value. Yet upon closer examination of the blocks, we see that they are outstanding contemporary works of art that exhibit a plethora of meanings and understandings.

Introduction

"Quilt-making takes me through a wonderfully breathtaking rite of passage. The experience is so beautiful; I continue to overflow with ideas, patterns, symbols, and colorful visions that can be shared with family, friends, and the world. My indigenous ancestors are with me the whole time I work. It is as if they are continuously reminding me of the responsibility I have to those who came before and those yet to come. I view myself as an instrument that continues the cycle of traditional art through wall covers, quilts, and wearable art."

—*Myrah Brown Green*

I remember using my mother's old Singer sewing machine when my legs grew long enough to reach the pedal. Our house was always filled with creative activities. Sewing was the one that became my passion. By the time I became a teenager, I was making my own clothes to wear to school; my babysitting pay went straight to the local fabric store.

Living in one of the country's most diverse cities—Cambridge, Massachusetts—my clothes began to reflect pieces of clothing indigenous to other parts of the world. I added Asia's Mandarin collars to my blouses, my skirts wrapped like those worn in Africa, and I stitched and beaded headbands inspired by Native American designs.

I sewed clothes for a number of years. When I moved to Brooklyn, New York, as an adult, I began experimenting with other types of fiber techniques: crochet, knitting, tatting, and quilting, making patterns and symbols the focus of the completed project. As an instructor, I developed an African textile printing, weaving, and embellishing course I taught at a local college. That course established my love for cultural symbols and symbolism.

Since that first experience with my mother's old Singer, I have embarked on a creative journey to find ways of fusing cultural world symbols with quilts, igniting creative sparks in the quilters I teach.

Not only does this book give you pieces and inspiration to create your own cultural quilts, but you'll also learn about the origins of the symbols and the culture that inspired each one.

WORLD'S LARGEST CLASSROOM

The symbols throughout this book have been drawn from a variety of countries on continents I have been fascinated with all of my life. The way others speak, look, wear clothing, prefer specific colors and patterns, and perform day-to-day tasks have all contributed to the inspiration for this book.

In these pages, you'll discover several cultural symbols found in Africa, Asia, Australia, Europe, North America, and South America. Not only does this book give you pieces and inspiration to create your own cultural quilts, but you'll also learn about the origins of the symbols and the culture that inspired each one. You'll also learn the basics of foundation piecing, a traditional technique that makes the job of piecing quilt blocks easier and more precise by sewing numbered pattern pieces onto a temporary background. And you'll have the chance to create your own pieced symbols using the patterns and step-by-step instructions provided.

Journey with me and experience the world's largest classroom. Enjoy the six continents of world symbols and begin experimenting with them to create your own one-of-a-kind quilts.

Myrah

Chapter 1

Getting Started

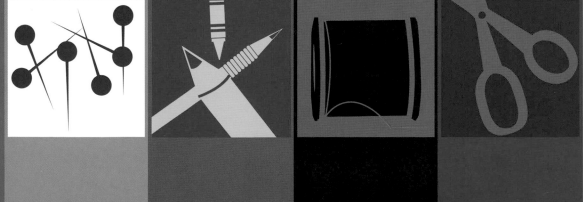

Foundation piecing, also referred to as paper piecing, is a quilting technique in which pieces of fabric are sewn onto a permanent or temporary backing that helps make your blocks easier to work with and assemble. This technique allows you to create precision pieced blocks without the fuss of matching points and set-in seams.

I am free-spirited when it comes to adding images in quilt tops. Many of my quilts are narrative in nature, with patches of quilt piecing included somewhere on the quilt top. When I piece those images or when I piece the quilt border, I like there to be some semblance of order. Foundation piecing is how I achieve that order.

On page 15, you'll find step-by-step instructions for foundation piecing a quilt block. You will discover that the fewer the number of pieces in the block, the easier it will be to complete. For this reason, you may want to choose a project such as the Ankh in Chapter 2 or the Heart in Chapter 7 before you move onto more complicated projects.

Before getting started, gather all of your supplies, thread your machine, and choose a short stitch setting (approximately 15-20 stitches per inch). You will not back stitch to lock your thread, so it's easier later to take out the stitching and keep the paper backing intact. Pre-wash your fabrics, and, if you are new to the foundation piecing technique, note that it's best to work with tightly woven 100-percent cotton fabric.

While you can use lightweight fabric such as muslin as your foundation material, my method calls for paper. The paper is temporary and can be torn away after the block is complete. Position the fabric on the foundation material, and then sew according to the assembly instructions provided. Keep a warm, dry iron nearby so that you can gently press open the seams as you sew.

I've provided the patterns in reverse because you'll sew the fabric pieces on the backside of the pattern. When the block is finished, it will be right side up and any directional design will show properly.

Choosing Fabric

When choosing quilt block symbols for your quilt, the right fabric can help the symbol in the block come alive. You don't have to choose African fabrics to make the African symbols. Colors, textures, and themes indigenous to the continent can make a difference. For example, rich indigo blue that contrasts with off-white similar to the color of muslin or a lighter blue can give you an African feel similar to Adire fabrics indigenous to the Yoruba people of Nigeria. Brown tones, including chocolates, tans, and mochas, can replicate the feel of mud cloth indigenous to those found in Mali. A little black or navy blue is always a vibrant choice when combined with a very saturated primary color, which is characteristic of Kente cloth.

Asian cloths have a visual richness, too. The symbols in the quilt blocks lend themselves well to Asian cotton prints and silks. A number of these fabrics can be found with small patterns indigenous to Asian culture. Asian metallic and a variety of hand-dyed fabrics including woven indigo blues, batiks, and tie-dyed cloths can make a spectacular block. Denim replicates the feel of indigo fabric, and is an easy-to-find alternative.

When it comes to the Australian continent, there are a number of Aboriginal-themed fabrics available in quilt shops today. Many have patterns that represent nature and the Aboriginal "Dreamings." The colors used to create these Australian-themed fabrics are predominantly shades of browns and greens, sometimes with a hint of primary colors like red, yellow, or blue. Footprints of birds, snakes, lizards, and handprints are common images printed on the cloth, as are spiral and other organic shapes.

Although most of the symbols in the Europe chapter are color specific, feel free to experiment with other hues. A heart motif is quite often seen in reds and pinks. If you want to stay within those families of colors, use stripes or polka dots in the red and pink color tones.

Experiment when creating Native American symbols. A variety of fabrics can be used for the feather block. The individual strands of a feather are usually on the diagonal. If you use a fabric print, cut the fabric on the diagonal or bias. This will give the illusion of a real feather. The types of fabrics that can help trick the eye are stripes, printed feather fabric, and colored, woven fabrics. You can also paint diagonal lines on the completed symbol to create a more realistic feather look.

South American fabrics are usually woven in rich colors, and embroidered cottons are popular, too. Using brightly colored fabrics for the block symbols will mimic the rich woven yarn-dyed fabrics indigenous to parts of South America known for their woven cloth.

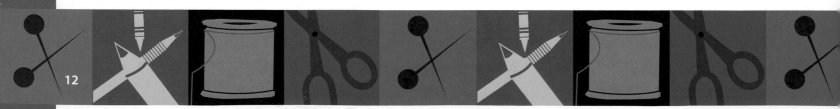

SUPPLIES

Foundation piecing can be machine or hand pieced. I have done both, depending on whether I have access to a sewing machine. However, I do the majority of foundation piecing by machine.

As you create more and more foundation-pieced quilt blocks, you will collect a variety of tools that you prefer to use. New and improved foundation piecing tools and materials are constantly being introduced to the quilt market. To develop a level of comfort with this technique, be open to experimenting with new tools.

The supplies that follow are what I prefer to use when foundation piecing by machine.

Copy machine or printer

Multiple copies of a pattern can be made on a photocopy machine. You can also scan the pattern and print it using a computer printer. All of the patterns in this book are provided in reverse so that once the block is complete, the image of the symbol will be facing the right direction.

Cutting mat

Self-healing cutting mats come in a variety of sizes and are readily available. When foundation piecing, I use a mat that fits on the work station next to my sewing machine.

Fabric

Various fabric types can be used once you have mastered the foundation piecing technique. I recommend beginning with tightly woven 100-percent cotton fabrics. Wash all fabrics before using them. Be careful when using scraps, as most are cut on the bias and therefore stretch more than usual.

Foundation material

There is a wide variety of foundation choices available. Permanent foundation choices include muslin and other lightweight cotton fabrics. Non-woven interfacing is another fine choice. I use only temporary foundations that I can remove from the back of the pieced fabrics. Once I have sandwiched the quilt top, the batting, and the back of the quilt in preparation for quilting, I find that there is less thickness without a permanent foundation. There are several temporary foundation materials on the market that can be used including copy paper, newsprint, smooth vellum, water-soluble paper, and pre-packaged foundation paper that also can be fed through most laser printers.

Marking tools

Pencils, pens, and colored pencils or crayons can be used to help you identify sections to stitch together. I like to use the colored tools to help me assign the pattern pieces to the fabric.

Quilt ruler

Most quilters use a 6" × 24" (15.2 × 61.0 cm) ruler. That length is not necessary when making a block. Since most of the foundation pattern pieces are less than 6" (15.2 cm), I like to use a quilter's ruler that is 6" × 12" (15.2 × 30.5 cm). It is wide enough to cover the width of most pattern pieces and long enough to cover most pieces that have been stitched together.

Rotary cutter

A rotary cutter works well when you are trimming the outside edge of the pattern pieces and have successfully cut them down to a ¼" (0.6 cm) seam allowance.

Scissors

I use a good pair of metal child's scissors. They are small and sharp enough to see the fabric pieces and blunt enough so you will not cut what you are not supposed to cut.

Sewing machine

Just about any sewing machine will do. When I am traveling and want to foundation piece, I take along a very small machine that only performs a straight stitch.

Straight pins

Use straight pins that will not get lost in the fabric and foundation material. I use long, sturdy, brightly colored glass head pins.

Thread

One hundred-percent cotton fabric thread in a neutral color is your best bet. When foundation piecing, the stitch length should be reduced since back stitching is not recommended. Choose a thread color that will blend with all of the fabrics in your quilt.

PIECING YOUR QUILT BLOCK

Instructions

Step 1: Color code each pattern piece with a crayon or pencil that matches its fabric color. Then, starting with A1, cut a piece of fabric large enough to cover the pattern piece (with the *wrong* side of the fabric), using the *unprinted* side of the pattern as a template (Fig. 1). You'll position and sew all fabric pieces on the unprinted side of the paper pattern. *Note:* Fabric should have at least ½"–1" (1.3–2.5 cm) excess all the way around. (You will trim all seams to ¼" (0.6 cm) after sewing.)

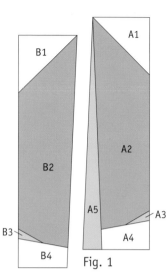

Fig. 1

Step 2: Next, place the A2 fabric piece over the A1 fabric piece, right sides together and completely covering the seam line between A1 and A2. Hold both fabrics along the seam allowance and open up the A2 fabric piece to make sure it extends around the entire A2 shape, plus at least ½" (1.3 cm) extra.

Step 3: Turn everything over so the paper pattern is up, and pin both fabrics in place (if necessary) on the paper side. Without backstitching, sew exactly on the seam line, beginning 2–3 stitches before the line begins and continuing 2–3 stitches after line ends.

Step 4: Remove pins, turn over, and gently press the seam open. Trim the seam to ¼" (0.6 cm). Open the A2 fabric so the right sides of both fabric pieces are exposed. Lay A3 next to pieces A1 and A2 at the seam line and repeat steps 2 and 3. Continue the process until Section A is complete.

Step 5: Complete Section B and each subsequent section until all sections are finished, referring to the assembly instructions (Fig. 2).

ASSEMBLY

Sew Section A to Section B

Fig. 2

Step 6: Press each section again and trim to a precise ¼" (0.6 cm) seam allowance around all sides. Stitch Section A to Section B, referring to the template (Fig. 3) when necessary.

Step 7: Gently press the completed block. Square off the finished block, leaving a ¼" (0.6 cm) seam allowance on all sides. Stay stitch using a straight stitch about ⅛" (0.3 cm) from the edge of the block. This prevents the stretching of fabric scraps that may have been cut on the bias. *Note:* Do not tear away the paper foundation until your quilt block is stay stitched. Your block is now ready to place in your quilt project.

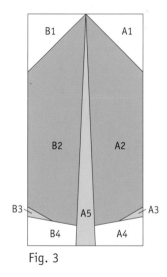

Fig. 3

15

Chapter 2

Africa

The richness of West African culture is evident in its textile tradition. Vibrant reds, deep blues, and bright greens all reflect the sun-kissed environment of the African continent. The indigo plant, a paste made from the cassava used to resist color, ore, and other natural elements native to the continent contribute to its textile legacy. Even the earth-toned textiles including bark cloth, kuba cloth, and bogolan mud cloths reflect the richness of colors found naturally in Africa's beautiful landscape. Since most of the symbols were created for a utilitarian purpose, they fall into one or more aspects of daily life: spiritual, rite of passage, or agricultural, to name a few.

Many of the traditional African symbols featured in this chapter originated in Egypt and countries in the western region of Africa. Symbols from these countries were accessible to the outside world primarily through barter, colonization, and the Trans-Atlantic Slave Trade. As different continents and countries were colonized, many symbols were taken back to Europe for study and use.

During the 1800s, when ethnographic museums were being developed, the symbols were taken to Britain in order to study the customs of African people. By 1925, European Modern artists began using African symbols in their work, which generally included paintings and sculpture.

The use of African symbols in the work of other artists subsequently spread to North America and other parts of the world. Egypt and the western region of Africa have always overflowed with symbols in sculpture, textiles, and paintings. These same symbols continue to surface today. Travel, the Internet, and published sources afford people the opportunity to access these age-old symbols.

The symbols in this chapter are as true to their visual form as possible. You can mix and match symbols within the chapter or combine symbols from other chapters when creating your quilts. There also is a cultural crossover for certain symbols. The Lotus Flower featured in this chapter, for example, is also indigenous to Asian culture. Quilt maker Susan Sato uses the Lotus Flower in her quilt "Japan by Way of Randall," referring to the flower as a water lily. Both flowers are usually referred to as one and the same in world folklore, despite some botanical differences.

6" × 6" (15.2 × 15.2 cm)

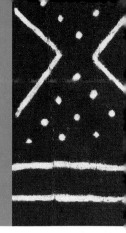

Ankh
"Eternal Life"

The Ankh is one of the world's oldest symbols, indigenous to ancient Egypt. The symbol appears as early as 2,500 Before Current Era and has been used as a descriptive element on pictographs, tomb paintings, and various statues of great kings and queens.

Ankh-shaped staffs were carried by pharaohs and gods. Those seen holding the Ankh were believed to be anointed with the power to give life or take life away. The Ankh signifies eternal life, immortality of the gods, and the key that unlocks the richness of the Nile River. When the Jews sojourned in Egypt, the Ankh was said to be the symbol placed on their doorposts during the Passover to depict life.

The Ankh was adopted as one of the most prevalent symbols in Egyptian cosmology. Ra, the god of the sun, is portrayed wearing the Ankh between two cobras, which reflected higher learning. The Ankh was also a symbol revered by the Greek scholar, Pythagoras. From the time he arrived in Egypt around 547 BCE, his 23-year stay afforded him the opportunity to study with, and learn from, great mathematicians indigenous to the land. Learning about Egyptian symbols and creating relationships between them and the mathematic formula he developed was Pythagoras' pastime. The Pythagorean Theory ($A^2 + B^2 = C^2$) may have been based on the Ankh.

The Ankh has become a significant part of popular culture in North America. Today, jewelers create charms and earrings in the likeness of the symbol. Many wear Ankh T-shirts and body tattoos.

CROSSING CULTURES

The early Christians in Egypt adopted the Ankh cross around the 4th century Current Era. To these Christians, who were members of the Coptic Church and active worshipers of a monolithic God, the Ankh cross stood for all things good and never-ending. As time moved forward, the Coptic Cross became the symbol of the church. Its visual appearance obviously has its foundation in the Ankh symbol. Like the Ankh symbol, the Coptic Cross represents eternal life.

See instructions for Ankh on page 86.

6" × 6" (15.2 × 15.2 cm)

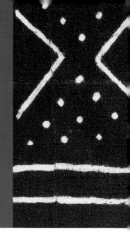

Eye of Heru
"Protection"

There are a number of symbols indigenous to Egyptians that have been handed down through the ages. The Eye of Heru is one of them. Its thick eyebrow and long tails extending from the eye seem to resemble the markings on a falcon's face. In Egyptian cosmology, Heru was identified with the head of a falcon.

The Eye of Heru is also known by a variety of names including Udjat, Eye of Horus, and All Seeing Eye. In addition to its power of divine protection, the Eye of Heru is believed to have the power to ward off sickness, bring wealth and fertility, and deflect negative energy.

Heru was immaculately conceived by his parents, Ausar and Auset. Ancient Egyptian religion reminds us that as an adult, Heru had one eye ripped out of his head and shattered during a battle with his jealous uncle, Set. Heru was protecting his father from Set's ignorance. Thoth, the god of magic and wisdom, traveled the world and beyond, finding 63 of the 64 pieces of Heru's eye. He then used his magical powers to recreate the missing piece, hence healing the Eye of Heru. Thoth's healing of the eye continues to represent protection, wealth, and healing.

CROSSING CULTURES

Variations of the Eye of Heru include the eye within a pyramid, associated with freemasonry and the United States dollar bill. Also, the original pharmacist's Rx symbol was an eye with an "x" below it. This version, used as recently as the 19th century, was inspired by the Eye of Heru. Some pharmacists today still use the variation in their logos.

The Eye of Heru is worn as a charm and talisman (objects believed to have spiritual properties) and is used to decorate other forms of manmade objects including furniture, wearable art, and quilts. It is believed that every object made requires some thought and design and that the thought reflects the culture that produced the object.

See instructions for Eye of Heru on page 88.

6" × 6" (15.2 × 15.2 cm)

Kanaga Crocodile
"Transition, Fruitfulness"

I have taken creative liberty to make what I call the Kanaga Crocodile. The symbol is inspired by the three-part wooden Kanaga mask made by the Dogon people of Mali, West Africa.

Professional craftsmen create Kanaga masks. Each craftsman ultimately becomes the wearer of his own mask once it is created. When an individual puts on the mask, he goes through a spiritual transformation. The ancestor spirit embodies the person who wears the mask, which is typically worn during large public ceremonial rituals to honor the deceased.

An old Dogon story tells us that the representation of the Kanaga mask is a crocodile that carried the original ancestors across a river and into the area of Mali, where the Dogon people now live. Ancestors play a very important role in African culture. The wearing of a mask links the ancestor realm to humankind.

When I look at the Kanaga mask, I see arms outstretched to heaven and legs facing downward to earth, and the center is a canal that brings us to earth when we are born and back to the heavens when we transcend.

CULTURES

In Ghana, West Africa, the crocodile is a revered symbol of the Asante people. The crocodile symbolizes adaptability because it lives in water and yet breathes air. One of the Adinkra symbols indigenous to Ghana's Asante people represents two crocodiles joined at the stomach. The joined crocodiles is a symbol of diversity, democracy, and unity of purpose.

CROSSING

See instructions for Kanaga Crocodile on page 90.

6" × 6" (15.2 × 15.2 cm)

Gye Nyame
"Except For God"

Indigenous to the Akan people of Ghana, West Africa, the Gye Nyame symbol is regarded as one of their highest spiritual symbols.

The symbol dates as far back as just before the 17th century Current Era. In Ghanaian folklore, it is said that "the great symbol dates back to time immemorial, no one lives who saw its beginning and no one will live to see its end, except for God."

This symbol represents the omnipotence, the omnipresence, and the immortality of God. It refers primarily to the magnitude of God while reflecting His influence over all of creation.

Gye Nyame is one of the most admired Adinkra symbols used by artists in North America. It appears as a decorative accent on a variety of crafts and other items including furniture, clothing, and fashion accessories.

Adinkra symbols, like the Gye Nyame, are usually stamped on a white, black, or very saturated colored cotton cloth using a carved calabash dipped in a black tar-like substance that is used as ink. The substance is made by boiling the bark of the badee tree that has been pounded by women in the Adinkra Stamping Village in the Ghanaian town of Kumasi.

CULTURES

Symbols that represent God are found throughout many cultures. Since Before the Current Era, Christianity has used the circle as one of its symbols to represent God and eternity because it has no beginning and no end. Three entwined circles represent the Trinity, symbolizing the undying Father, Son, and Holy Spirit.

CROSSING

See instructions for Gye Nyame on page 92.

6" × 6" (15.2 × 15.2 cm)

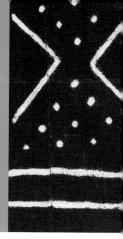

Lotus Flower
"Renewal, Rebirth"

The Lotus Flower is one of my favorite symbols, probably because of the way it begins its life. The lotus starts as a seed in a muddy environment at the bottom of a water source. As the flower grows, it moves toward the sun until it floats to the top of the water and blooms.

Ancient Egyptians held the lotus flower in high esteem. Sesen, the Egyptian name for the lotus flower, is usually white or pink with more than a dozen spreading oval-shaped petals. Ancient Egyptians believed that because the lotus flower closes at night, submerges itself under water, and then reappears in the morning, it symbolizes the sun, creation, and rebirth.

One of the Egyptian creation stories tells us that at the beginning of time, a larger-than-life lotus flower arose from watery chaos and gave birth to the sun on the first day. The lotus flower appears quite often in Egyptian art held by or adorning humans and gods. Since the fourth dynasty, Egyptians have used the lotus flower in religious ceremonies and funerals, probably because of its growth process.

The Lotus Flower also symbolizes purity. The flower comes in a variety of colors, but white is the most common. In Buddhist cosmology, it is said that the lotus is the first flower that bloomed in the universe. Whether this is myth or reality, the lotus maintains its place in plant cultivation as the flower that is known not only for its beauty, but also by the process of its growth.

CROSSING CULTURES

The growth process of the lotus is considered by some to be a metaphor for the journey of life. Many Asian religions, especially those throughout India, believe that the muddy darkness represents our inability to clearly see life's path. Moving toward the sun is the process of gaining clarity. When the lotus flower floats to the top of the water and blooms, some believe it represents an individual who has reached spiritual growth and enlightenment.

See instructions for Lotus Flower on page 94.

Sacred Symbols #1

In "Sacred Symbols #1," Michelle Lewis uses the Kanaga Crocodile as a medallion in the center of her quilt. The Kanaga Crocodile gives the quilt a taste of Africa while the appliqué motif frames the symbol. Commercial batik fabrics indigenous to Indonesia are used as the foundation fabrics of the quilt. The cowry shells sewn on as the eyes of the crocodile are indigenous to the Polynesian Islands and Africa. The shell of the cowry has been used for money and spiritual rituals in parts of Africa, southern Asia, and the South Pacific. History tells us that ships were docked using huge bundles of cowry shells as weights. The cowry shells were indigenous to the Polynesian Islands before they came to Africa via large merchant ships.

40" × 41" (101.6 × 104.1 cm)
2005
Michelle Lewis

28

Summertime

35" × 36½"
(88.9 × 92.7 cm)
2008
Myrah Brown Green

In June 2008, I was blessed to become the proud grandmother of my first grandchild, Summer-Zaire, who I affectionately call "Summertime." We knew she was a girl before her birth. We also knew what she would be named so that the family could connect and properly welcome her into the world. Her quilt had to have just the right symbols. The Ankh and the Goddess symbols (featured in Chapter 7) were my first choice. Both are symbols of life. I want some of her first symbols of knowledge to represent fruitful living and a sense of self. Even though I knew I wanted to use pink in the quilt, I did not want it to be such a traditional girly one so I added green and purple. In the pink sashing, I quilted the Feather symbol found in Chapter 5.

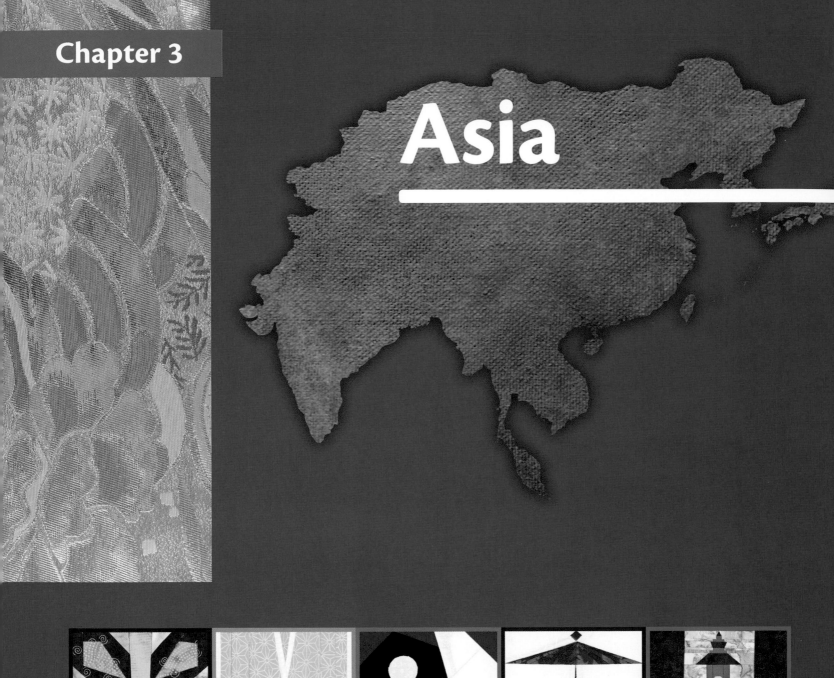

Chapter 3

Asia

Even in the midst of today's growing technology and the hustle and bustle of everyday living, those who reside on the Asian continent maintain an order between humanity and nature. This "way" may be attributed to the rich legacy left behind by Asian ancestors, who had a great respect for antiquity and the lessons that were taught over the centuries. Asian symbols grew out of philosophy and painting, nature and spirituality, and the human world. Architecture and dress also influenced Asian symbols.

These symbols have always had a place in Asian culture. Each symbol maintained its role and performed the specific duty it was meant to perform. Customs and various types of Asian rites set the tone for how the symbols were developed and then characterized. Few symbols were forgotten over the years but many were translated into different forms like the pagoda, which was built first as an "early stupa temple," later referred to as the "later stupa temple," and then the "watchtower," the "stone pagoda" (featured in this chapter), and finally the "wooden pagoda."

Asia consists of many different ethnic groups. Its art, music, cuisine, and literature are important parts of Asian culture. The use of Asian symbols among its people goes hand in hand with the human "self" or "mind." How the people use the symbols dictates how their circumstances ultimately impact a myriad of personal and community relations, and also self-awareness. The multitude of symbols indigenous to the Asian continent serve as a medium that raises the level of consciousness of an intellectual people on a daily basis. This type of interplay with the Asian symbol and the human "self" has spilled over into other cultures around the world.

Religion and Eastern philosophy also play an important role in the culture. Buddhism, Hinduism, Daoism, Taoism, Confucianism, Islam, and Christianity make up the continent's spiritual richness.

Although Asia has maintained an abundance of its ancient cultural traditions, Western culture has infused some of its own ways due to trade, the Internet, travel, and other means of contact.

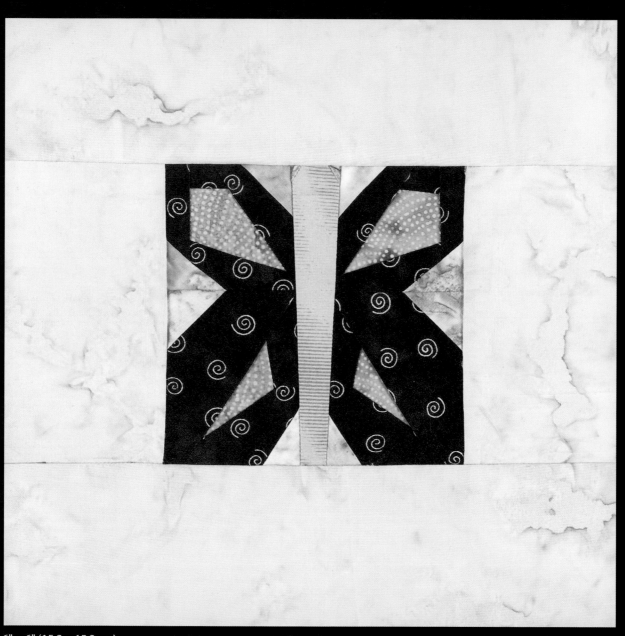

6" × 6" (15.2 × 15.2 cm)

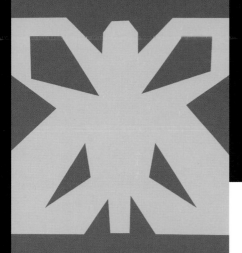

Butterfly
"Transformation"

The butterfly is one of the most symbolic creatures in nature. Human beings enjoy observing its graceful demeanor and fanciful archetype so much that it has become a favorite insect of many. Throughout the vast number of Asian cultures, the Butterfly has been considered a symbol of new life, spiritual evolution, and prosperity. Butterflies appear to meditate as they perch on flowers and foliage for minutes at a time.

To Buddhists, the butterfly represents an independent soul that remains unfamiliar with affection because it survives independently from its mother. Unlike many living creatures that begin life through the nurturing of their mother, the butterfly transitions through life on its own.

The Japanese also believe that a single butterfly is a symbol of young womanhood, and two symbolize a successful marriage. Jade butterflies carved by Asian artisans represent triumphant love.

In China, the Butterfly symbol represents undying love, especially for the young at heart. The Chinese also believe that the Butterfly embroidered on clothing or personal belongings can serve as a source of empowerment.

CROSSING CULTURES

Christians have revered the Butterfly as a symbol of transformation because of its three stages of metamorphosis, from the caterpillar to the cocoon and finally to the butterfly. In this instance, the butterfly becomes the symbol of resurrection. Many images of the Garden of Eden depict the soul of Adam with the wings of a butterfly. Paintings that show butterflies along with the Madonna and Child symbolize their care for the human soul.

See instructions for Butterfly on page 96.

6" × 6" (15.2 × 15.2 cm)

Kimono
"Femininity, Protection"

Kimono, which in Japanese translates to "the thing worn," was made popular in Japan during the 19th century. It is a formal garment that was influenced by the West, and gradually became a traditional symbol of Japan. The Heian period, which lasted from 794 to 1185 CE, forced women to cover themselves with layers of clothing. The kimono provided a way for women to express themselves through the colors and print of the fabric.

The kimono is traditionally a heavy garment. It has an inner layer with many colors and patterns. This construction symbolizes virtue and beauty. Today's more contemporary Japan has removed the kimono from everyday life. It is now a garment symbolically worn by both men and women during the holidays and on special occasions.

The kimono is also worn for rites of passages and 20th birthday celebrations. It is a symbol in Japanese culture that represents peace and tranquility.

CULTURES

The kimono also appears in the United States, and has been adopted by American women and men as a symbol of royalty and personal attachment to the Japanese culture. It was made popular after the release of the 2005 film, *Memoirs of a Geisha*, and has been reproduced in many styles, fabrics, and colors.

CROSSING

See instructions for Kimono on page 98.

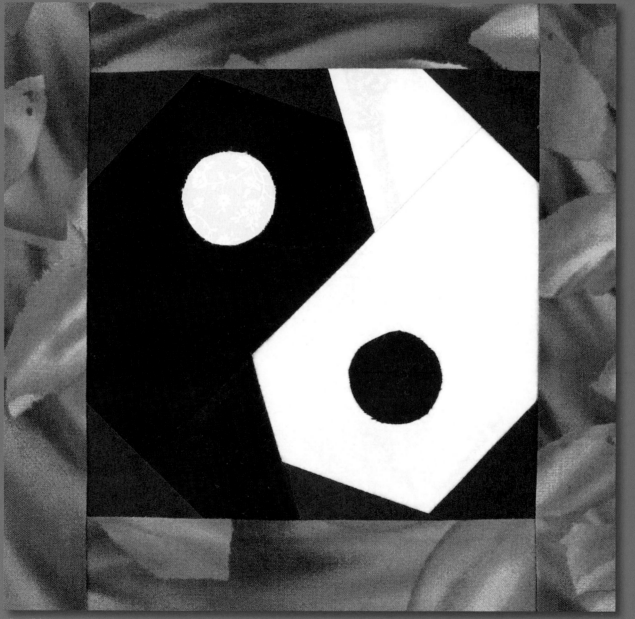

6" × 6" (15.2 × 15.2 cm)

Yin & Yang
"Male-Female, Duality, Balance"

The Yin and Yang symbol was first believed to have appeared between 1,300 and 1,200 BCE, during China's Southern Song Dynasty. During this time, Chinese art and philosophy paralleled one another. Rational and intellectual thoughts were interchanged with the emotional. The tangible was interchanged with the intangible. The symbol became a visual manifestation of this process, called "unity in duality."

The circular symbol is perfectly divided into two parts. One side is a light color and the other side is dark. The two sides are opposites but also complete each other, creating an observable experience in the form of an object or process. The unity of the two opposing sides is represented by two small circles. In the light side of the symbol, a dark circle is present. In the dark side, there is a light circle.

Examples of dual relationships are masculine and feminine, positive and negative, up and down, and right and wrong. All of these relationships are symbiotic; each is necessary for the other to function.

The Yin and Yang symbol most commonly appears in black and white. However, a variety of fabrics in multiple colors and patterns can be used as long as one side is light and the other is dark.

CROSSING CULTURES

The "unity in duality" philosophy is a universal concept that transcends Asian cultures, becoming quite popular in many cultures throughout the world. The Yin and Yang symbol appears in a variety of Asian cultures including Japanese, Korean, and Vietnamese. In Japan, dual qualities of Yin and Yang parallel its in-yo symbol, which means "The Way of Yin and Yang." The Yin and Yang became the center image of the South Korean flag in the late 19th century. In Vietnam, the symbol appears in and around Buddhist temples where Chinese culture has significant influence.

See instructions for Yin & Yang on page 100.

6" × 6" (15.2 × 15.2 cm)

Parasol
"Protection, Status"

Parasols have been around for thousands of years. The parasol is an umbrella, which was traditionally an Indian symbol of protection and royalty before it expanded to other cultures.

The Parasol represents protection from the heat of suffering, desire, obstacles, illness, and harmful forces. It has also symbolized wealth and status. When a person's entourage was approached, the more influential the person was, the more parasols were seen in the group.

Indian Buddhists, who envisioned Buddha as their spiritual leader, used the parasol to protect him. Buddhists adopted the Asian tradition of 13 stacked parasols, which defined the status of a king or queen. Buddhist mythology tells us that the King of Nagas (serpent-like creatures) gave the Buddha a heavily embellished parasol.

CULTURES CROSSING

The Parasol symbol is represented in the art of many cultures, including Ancient Greece and Rome, China, Meso America, the Middle East, and North Africa. It has also been given other uses. In Ancient Egypt, the parasol represents religious symbolism. It has been closely associated with Osiris, the bringer of rain, who is the son of Nut and god of the underworld. Parasols were also tied to the Victorian era because women preferred pale skin. They symbolized the separation between ladies with means and working-class women.

See instructions for Parasol on page 102.

6" × 12" (15.2 × 30.5 cm)

Pagoda
"Spiritual Enlightenment"

A pagoda is a sacred building indigenous to Indian culture that was adopted by the Buddhist tradition. The pagoda, a structural component in a community of temples, was used to bury the bones of the cremated remains of the deceased.

This architectural creation's origin in India dates as far back as the 6th century BCE, before Buddhism began. People continued to worship the pagoda, especially after Buddhism was formed. Once Buddhism emerged, the pagoda, used for Indian tombs, was called a "stupa." The stupa was shaped like a dome and made primarily from stone or soil. Before Buddha died, he asked his students to have his bones buried in one such structure.

The stupa became the symbol of the tomb of Buddha and the most important structure in the temple community. The architectural form of the pagoda began to evolve into what it is today when the Indians inserted a pole through the center of the dome from the top of the structure to the earth. Indian culture believed the pole represented the center of the universe, controlling the birth of everything.

The Pagoda's tiered structure symbolizes progressive stages of spiritual enlightenment. The tiers rising in diminishing scale represent the axis linking earth and sky. Each set of tiers ranges in number from two to more than five.

CROSSING CULTURES

The pyramids of Egypt were used as a sacred form of architecture to bury the deceased. Like the Buddha's pagoda, pyramids were built to house the remains and personal possessions of important Egyptians, usually kings and queens. The Kota people of Gabon, Africa, built burial structures where they placed bundles of bones. The bundles were embellished with a reliquary mask made specifically for each of the deceased.

See instructions for Pagoda on page 104.

Japan by Way of Randall

Susan Sato is a third-generation Japanese-American quilter always on the lookout for new Asian patterns. She saw the pieced symbols that I had created and was inspired to make a wall hanging. The Pagoda symbol, which represents spiritual enlightenment, needed to be the center of attention with hand-dyed fabrics in the windows. The Parasol and Lotus blocks were pieced using Japanese fabrics from the quilt maker's stash, balancing the quilt layout. Sashiko (Japanese style of quilting), along with traditional quilting stitches, were used for visual impact. Beads, buttons, and metallic threads add texture. The title of Sato's quilt came from her husband, Randy, who would walk by her design wall and comment on color placement and balance.

17¾" × 23⅛"
(45.1 × 58.7 cm)
2006
Susan Sato

Oriental Butterflies

19½" × 16¾" (49.6 × 42.5 cm)
2006
Debbie Markowitz

Quilt maker Debbie Markowitz used the Butterfly as the focal point of "Oriental Butterflies." The Kimono and Parasol blocks complement the Asian-themed quilt. The Butterfly at the far left has been appliquéd in a three-dimensional fashion, achieved with a stiff interfacing that gives the Butterfly the appearance of being in flight. It has been stitched at its center so that its wings can move freely. The pale green in the background gives softness to the quilt top. The symbols seem to be almost floating.

Chapter 4

Australia

A number of Australian-themed fabrics are being sold in quilt shops. The designs are inspired by images created by indigenous Australians, also known as Aboriginal people.

Original artwork by the Aborigines was painted in the desert sand during "Dreamings," recorded journeys traveled by the Ancestor Spirits throughout the land. These records show how the Ancestor Spirits formed all living things, interacted with beings, and laid down and practiced the laws. In the Dreaming state, one connects with collective myths, symbols, primordial elements, and creative literary and artistic foundations. Dreamings can be manifested in the form of tangible creations including paintings, sculpture, and journals. The images were used to outline, support, and teach an individual or group's belief system.

Through stories, Dreamings covered a variety of themes and symbols. They are an intricate system of information, faith, and customs derived from stories of creation, relationships, and spirituality that embodies and informs all spiritual and physical aspects of an indigenous Australian's life. Totemic representations of animals, foliage, and other natural symbols regarded as religious icons were carved and painted, too.

The Aborigines first inhabited the Australian continent more than 40,000 years ago. European explorers including the Dutch, Portuguese, and Spanish did not make contact with Australia until the 17th century. When the continental drift occurred, Australia was one of the only continents that developed independently. As time moved forward, the people spoke a variety of indigenous languages and dialects. Because of Australia's isolation, the cultural traditions of the people reflect their deep connection with the land.

Today, traditional representations of Aboriginal Dreamings and totemic symbols have been replaced by paintings on canvas. Although Australia has been inhabited by Europeans and other cultures from around the world, Aboriginal traditions and symbols still maintain a strong presence on the continent.

6" × 18" (15.2 × 45.7 cm)

Sacred Totem
"Family, Identity, Ancestry"

Every family member or individual of a clan who follows Australia's Aboriginal customs is born into a totem. A totem marks the resting place of ancestors and other special beings whose spirits live on. These totemic places are sacred spaces found throughout different parts of Australia.

The totem gives men and women an individual identity and connects them with the natural world. The totem also plants the individual into a rich cultural tradition that enforces ties and responsibilities to the land and teaches men and women who they are as descendents of Aboriginal people.

All totems are marked by symbols of any living creature or element of the universe including humans, animals, the earth, sun, lightning, rain, stars, sky, and the moon.

As this pieced symbol is somewhat complicated, refer to the whole pattern diagram quite often. This will keep you on track when sewing sections together.

CROSSING CULTURES

Northwest Coastal groups indigenous to North America, including the Kwakiutl, Haida, and Coast Salish, built totem poles. These tall, narrow wooden structures represented the history of the family living on the property where they stood. Symbols carved into the totem pole included animals such as the raven, bear, and wolf and a variety of fish. The symbols chosen represented the family lineage and served as a reminder of family history to descendents yet to come.

See instructions for Sacred Totem on page 108.

6" × 6" (15.2 × 15.2 cm)

Lightning Spirit Ancestor
"Thunder, Lightning, Codes of Conduct"

When the rainy season begins in Australia, the Lightning Spirit flies into the sky and sits on storm clouds, sending out sounds of thunder and strikes of lightning. Watching the people below, he makes sure that the Aboriginals are living the traditions of their ancestors. Those traditions include sacred ceremonies, passing on their history and culture to the next generation, and practicing good codes of conduct.

Stories like this are indigenous to the Aboriginals, who believe that they have lived since the beginning of time and with them, throughout each generation, came spirit ancestors that trace the lineage of their ancestors. The spirit ancestors, like the Lightning Spirit Ancestor, are remembered during a Dreaming practiced by the Aboriginal people. Those who experience Dreamings can speak about the creation of the world and its universe, the development of human beings, and the responsibilities that humans have to their lineage and their society.

The Lightning Spirit Ancestor is also a symbol of fertility, which is synonymous with creativity. Lightning is seen among some Aboriginal Australians as destructive because people or places struck by lightning can be harmed.

Even though the Lightning Spirit Ancestor is an Aboriginal "Dream" spirit, it appears as male or female to impart its lessons. Use a skin-colored fabric of choice to represent your lineage.

CULTURES

The lightning deity Tlaloc was important in Mexico's Aztec culture during the 15th and 16th centuries. Tlaloc was known to use flashes of light in the sky to send spirits to the Aztec heaven.

CROSSING

See instructions for Lightning Spirit Ancestor on page 114.

6" × 6" (15.2 × 15.2 cm)

Rainbow Serpent
"Duality: Creativity and Destruction"

One of the most popular Aboriginal spirit ancestors is the Rainbow Serpent. Present during many Dreamings, the Rainbow Serpent is a snake-like being whose dual spirit is both creative and destructive. It is a protector of its people and the land on which it lives. However, it can destroy anyone or anything when respect is not shown to it or to the world.

The Rainbow Serpent, through Dreamings, is usually linked with water sources such as rivers, streams, and lakes. Aboriginal folklore tells us that the Lightning Spirit Ancestor traveled to make lightning in the sky and the Rainbow Spirit Ancestor followed to sit on a cloud so that it would rain.

The Rainbow Serpent is a very old Aboriginal symbol. It has been found on cave walls and rock paintings as early as 4,000 BCE. Today's contemporary Aboriginal artists continue to use the Rainbow Serpent in many of their paintings and sculptures, adding personal motifs to the body of this creature. The motifs represent designs indigenous to the clan or community of the individual artist.

Rainbow Serpents as spirit ancestors continue to be revered by the Aboriginal people of Australia. Their images contribute to the spiritual forces that connect artists to the land in which they belong.

CULTURES

The serpent as a symbol representing protection has been used for many years in the Asian culture. Mucalinda, who in his original existence was human, transformed into the king of serpents to protect Buddha from torrential rains as he meditated under a tree. Mucalinda believed that protecting Buddha was protecting the one who guarded humankind. Once the storm ended, Mucalinda resumed his human form and his life as a king.

CROSSING

See instructions for Rainbow Serpent on page 117.

Dreaming Down Under

"Dreaming Down Under" appears to take the visual form of an Aboriginal Dreaming. Aboriginal artists still maintain the ancient culture through paintings, journal writing, and storytelling. Betsy True uses the Rainbow Serpent and Lightning Spirit Ancestor blocks in this quilt. All of these symbols, indigenous to Aboriginal culture, come alive during "Dreamtime," a way that the indigenous Aboriginal connects with the ancestors throughout time so that the true traditions of the culture can be maintained. The hair of the Lightning Spirit Ancestors who sit in the center of the quilt seems to be moving just as lightning does. The earth-tone colors are reminders of Australia's natural environment.

32½" × 39"
(82.5 × 99.1 cm)
2006
Betsy True

Mother Ancestor Spirits

42" × 36" (106.7 × 91.4 cm)
2008
Myrah Brown Green

Many of my quilts feature female images. Some are dancing, some are singing, while others are in meditation. Most of the women are my ancestors. The Sacred Totem ancestor in "Mother Ancestor Spirits" represents my ancestor lineage of women. My maternal and paternal grandmothers and their mothers and the mothers of their mothers are represented in this quilt. The Sacred Totem is a totemic figure usually marked in a totem pole to signify a specific family lineage. When creating "Mother Ancestor Spirits," I found myself envisioning my women relatives standing in a row, imparting advice and wisdom I can pass on to my daughters.

Chapter 5

North

America

When I was a young student in elementary school, I was taught that North America was a "melting pot." I didn't understand until I was older that an analogy was being made between food and the cultures that inhabit this rich continent.

North America is indeed a melting pot of cultures from around the globe. The languages, customs, and symbols of North America reflect the people indigenous to the continent, immigrants who came to stay, and visitors just passing through.

Life in North America can be reliably dated before 11,500 BCE. Its early development of symbols is based on the influence of indigenous North Americans, many who ended up on the continent as a result of the precontinental drift, when the entire globe was contiguously joined together. The influence of the Mayans found in Central America traveled north to spark the development of the Aztecs, Hopi, and other groups indigenous to the southern part of North America long before they flourished from 3,000 BCE to 1,500 CE.

These early groups were responsible for the domestication of crops now used around the world including corn, squash, and tomatoes.

Although documented sources tell us that there was very little contact between North American people and the outside world before 1492, the contact that did occur was substantial. The idea of North America as a melting pot is evident in many of the symbols found throughout the continent. African Adinkra symbols are visible in ironwork designs used in windows and gates on houses. The Washington Monument in Washington, D.C., is modeled after an Egyptian obelisk. Oscar, the Academy award, significantly resembles the Egyptian god of creativity, Ptah.

North American cultures continue to reinvent new symbols and recycle old ones. The "melting pot" my childhood teacher talked about has become even larger. Our ancestors, indigenous North Americans, and those who came from other parts of the world in search of new beginnings left legacies that intertwine, creating new legacies and new symbols.

3" × 6" (7.6 × 15.2 cm)

Kachina
"Guidance, Order"

Six months of the year, the Kachina lives among the Hopi people, Native Americans who reside primarily on the mesas of Arizona. Kachinas, believed by the Hopi people to be spirits that serve as intermediaries between the gods and human beings, first made their appearance on Hopi mesas in the mid-1800s.

At the start of the winter solstice, initiated Hopi men from the community impersonate the Kachina by wearing a masked costume that embodies the spirit of a particular guardian. The inaugural ceremony of this season is called the Powamu. The ceremony highlights the Kachina's presence by teaching boys and girls about the Kachina as a spirit, guardian, helper, and symbol of the invisible world.

During this ceremony, a variety of Kachinas with names like Owl, Corn Maiden, Eagle, and White Buffalo bear unique powers similar to the attribute after which they were named. The initiated men travel throughout the community, dancing at religious ceremonies and visiting children in their homes. The purpose of their visits is to remind the children to behave, to maintain order, and to leave a doll carved in the image of the Kachina that will help the children recognize and remember their guardian spirits.

One of the most popular Kachina guardian spirits is called Soyoko, or Ogre Woman. Although her presence frightens the children, Soyoko's purpose is to remind them to respect their elders and maintain the Hopi tradition.

CULTURES

CROSSING

The Kachina is only indigenous to Native American culture, predominantly the Hopi and Zuni nations. However, the Egungun ancestor spirit, indigenous to the Yoruba people of Nigeria, West Africa, functions similarly. Like the Kachina, the Egungun association is a group of initiated individuals whose main purpose is to honor ancestors and call on their guidance and protection. Their colorful costumes are elaborately pieced, combining the rich traditional stripped textile technique of Africa with cloths indigenous to the country.

See instructions for Kachina on page 120.

57

3" × 6" (7.6 × 15.2 cm)

Feather
"Ascension, Spirituality, Evolution"

The Feather is a Native American symbol that represents ascension and spiritual evolution. It also is a symbol of prayer and a mark of honor.

The feather was an adornment worn by Native American chiefs as early as 9,500 BCE to symbolize celestial wisdom. A chief wearing a feather was expected to have the ability to communicate with spirits. The feather allowed the chiefs to obtain answers from a higher plane.

Feathers worn by Native Americans are taken from birds that may have attributes similar to those needed by the wearer. For example, because geese are known to fly long distances, the goose feather is used to fledge an arrow. The eagle, one of the Native American's most esteemed birds, represents honor and a way to connect with the Supreme Being, or the Creator. Turkey feathers are most commonly used to decorate the Hopi Kachina masks.

Native Americans also believed that the Feather depicted the power of the thunder gods and the element air. The native people, referred to as pueblos, would use the Feather as a symbol of the cosmos and a talisman to provoke the rain. They would have to dance with the Feather in order to enhance this power.

CROSSING CULTURES

The Feather is also a Celtic, Egyptian, and Christian symbol. In Celtic culture, the feather adorned ornate robes worn by Druids. During Celtic rituals, the Druids, who were priests, judges, and academics of the time, wore feathered robes to connect with the sky gods and to learn more about the universe.

The Egyptians believed that the Feather was a symbol of the sky gods as well. In addition, Ma'at, the Egyptian Goddess of justice, used the feather to weigh the hearts of the newly dead in the underworld. Ma'at believed that the feather could determine the worthiness of a person's soul. Lastly, in the Christian faith, the feather represents virtues. Feathers were made into signet rings, which symbolized charity, hope, and faith. These rings were to be worn by a virtuous soul.

See instructions for Feather on page 122.

6" × 6" (15.2 × 15.2 cm)

60

Kokopelli
"Fertility, Prosperity"

Kokopelli, the humpbacked flute-playing figure, is common in ancient Native American stories. The image has been found on American rock carvings as early as the 15th century.

The word Kokopelli is derived from the Hopi word "kokopilau," which loosely translates as "wooden hump"; "koko" means wood and "pilau" means hump. Although the Kokopelli word comes from the Hopi culture, it is shared among other Native American groups. The Kokopelli figure carries a pouch of seeds on his back and has long antler-like hair. Both the seeds and antlers represent fertility and growth.

In Native American folklore, Kokopelli enters a town with a bag on his back playing a flute-like instrument. He dances across the town, making his presence known to all who reside there. Kokopelli's stay is not long but his power to spread fertility is lasting. It is believed that women who have longed to bear children will be blessed with the ability to do so after coming in contact with Kokopelli.

The Kokopelli symbol is also closely associated with rain, prosperity, and even marriage.

CROSSING CULTURES

Like Kokopelli, the Akuabaa, indigenous to the Asante people of Ghana, West Africa, represents fertility. In Ghanaian folklore, Akua and her husband longed to bear a child. Akua traveled miles and miles to a doctor who she had heard could help her. The doctor was able to help Akua and she did in fact bear a child. A wooden doll-like symbol named after Akua, called Akuabaa, was carved for her. The Akuabaa symbol protected Akua's unborn child and guided Akua through her pregnancy and into a safe delivery.

See instructions for Kokopelli on page 123.

Kachina & Feathers

The fabrics in this small quilt were just waiting for the Kachina! A couple years ago, quilt maker Sally Field had set aside a collection of turquoise and copper fabrics that needed the right project to make them shine. Even with paper piecing, they were not easy to work with. The dark blue/black around the Kachina is a stiff, heavy, inexpensive velvet from a surplus/salvage store. The copper fabric, used to make the leaf veins and stems, needed to be stabilized; neither of them wanted to adhere to straight seams. The black between the Kachina and Feathers is chenille from a local sporting goods store used to outline the Kachina and to give it and the Feathers their own space. Copper pony beads dangle from the chenille in the upper corners.

14¾" × 20¼"
(37.5 × 51.4 cm)
2006
Sally K. Field

Cindy Simms was raised in a quilting family on both sides and was taught the art of traditional patterns and quilting techniques at an early age. One of those techniques was foundation piecing on muslin. Today, everyone is taught that same technique but many choose paper instead of muslin. Simms chose the Native American theme because it is part of her family heritage. "Harvest Shield" is a quilt designed around the idea of a dream catcher, a traditional Native American charm that hangs over the bed of sleeping children to protect them from bad dreams. Simms' design moves in a circle. She incorporated feather charms to complement the Feather symbols in the quilt. These charms hang like the feathers found on a traditional dream catcher.

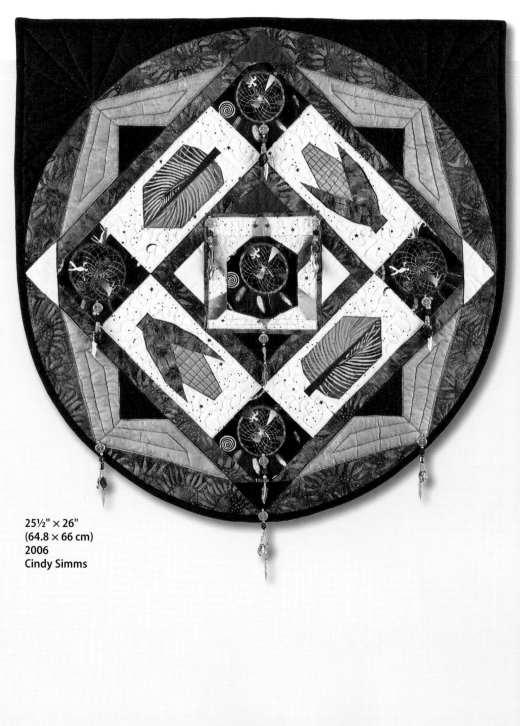

25½" × 26"
(64.8 × 66 cm)
2006
Cindy Simms

Chapter 6

South
America

South America is as rich as the cultures that inhabit it. Colombia, Brazil, Chile, Paracas, Nazca, Mocha, and the Central Andes, which is primarily present-day Peru and Bolivia, all contribute artistic traditions and symbolism to the continent. South America's land mass has dramatic contrast; on the west, its narrow coastal plain is bordered by the Pacific Ocean, and on the east, part of the Andes has one of the driest deserts in the world. Although South America produces a variety of crafts, it is known for its textile arts.

The Central Andes is one of the best-known areas on the continent. Its mountains divide a number of the South American countries into separate territories including the mountains, the Amazon basin, the valleys, and the coast. Because of this separation, each community has developed its own style of arts and crafts based on the accessibility of supplies indigenous to the area. Andean textiles are one of the oldest woven South American cloths. Andean tapestry appeared in Peru around 900 BCE. This weaving technique was used to make cloth during the next thousand years.

Andean grasslands are home to a variety of animals including alpacas, vicunas, guanacos, and the llama. These animals have served South American cultures for thousands of years, supplying people with labor, food to eat, and wool. The llama, in particular, has been treasured so much by the Andean culture that it has become one of their staple textile decorations.

Most South Americans identify with symbols and colors indigenous to their community. Each symbol is a source of pride and identity for each group. The Paracas culture, best known for its beautiful textiles, flourished around 1,000 BCE to about 200 CE on the southern coast of Peru. Unlike the woven designs in Andean textiles, Paracas designs were predominantly embroidered symbols of dancers, warriors, and birdlike creatures.

South American cultures have contributed a rich legacy to the world of arts and crafts, especially textiles. Woven blankets, mantel scarves, felted and knitted sweaters, and other textile crafts have become popular in North American communities.

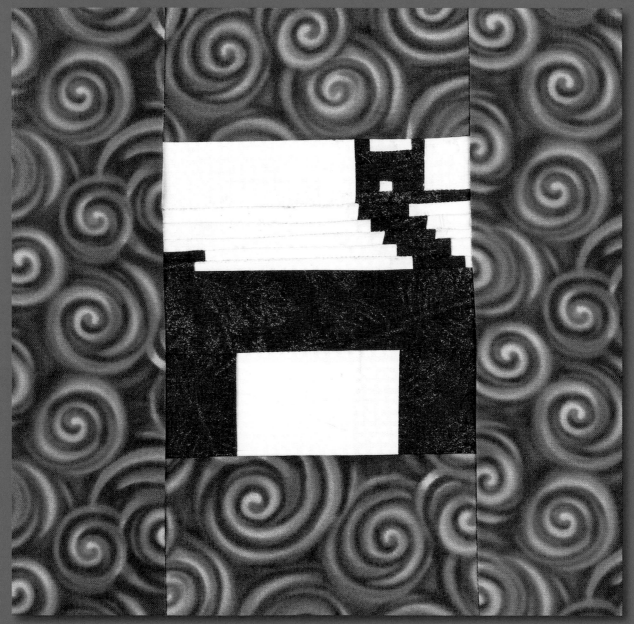

6" × 6" (15.2 × 15.2 cm)

Llama
"Endurance, Responsibility, Hard Work"

The llama is one of the four members of the camel family. Although it flourished in North America more than 12,000 years ago, the llama is most revered on the South American continent. This fully domesticated animal is considered a hard worker because its level of determination when burdened far outweighs most others.

The llama is a symbol of endurance, responsibility, strenuous work, and perseverance in reaching a goal. South American cultures respect the llama so much that its image is woven into a large majority of their indigenous textiles.

A great deal of attention has been paid to the llama by pre-Inca civilizations and the Incas themselves. Llamas were bred for labor to use when building their communities. Early dynasties revered the llama as a divine symbol when worshipping the sun in the temples these animals helped to build. Llamas were also used as offerings to deities. Male llamas were the most valuable, while female llamas with and without offspring were not as significant.

The Llama symbol continues to be used as an image integrated into an assortment of cloths indigenous to South American cultures. Llamas teach us to climb slowly and securely in our endeavors, while examining whether we are being stubborn or cautious in our actions.

CROSSING CULTURES

At the time of the most recent ice age and its continental drift around 10,000 BCE, the llama left the North American continent. One particular group ended up in Asia and North Africa, which precipitated the need for a change in body type that would enable them to sustain themselves in a desert environment and obtain their food from vegetation that grew at a higher altitude. These llamas evolved into the camel. Another group ended up in South America, where they settled predominantly in Chile and Peru.

See instructions for Llama on page 126.

6" × 6" (15.2 × 15.2 cm)

Nanuma Duck
"Mother Earth, Nurturing"

S ymbols have been woven into textiles indigenous to South America's Andean culture since the pre-Columbian era. These textiles and the symbols woven into them serve as a gauge for societal development. The pre-Columbian period (any time before 1492) is defined as the time before Christopher Columbus made contact with indigenous cultures.

Many of the textiles and textile remnants created during this time period are some of the only surviving references of indigenous Andean social structure, ritual and spiritual practices, economic development, and other traditional habits practiced within the society. Nanuma, the duck symbol of Mother Earth, is one of them.

Nanuma was not woven into Andean textiles as often as the sun or Planet Venus symbols. However, Nanuma's role as Mother Earth was of great importance. The Mother Earth symbol teaches us about South America's rich landscape. This feminine principle is one of fertility, reproduction, and nourishment and includes all things that come from Mother Earth and the ancestors who have returned to her.

Create a collection of Nanuma ducks in a variety of sizes. The duck relationships can be the Mother Earth with her children. There can be a group of women Nanuma ducks who are sisters or they can represent friends. As a single symbol, dress her by appliquéing patterns to the body to give the hint of a garment.

CROSSING CULTURES

In China, the duck, usually of the Mandarin species, is used as a symbol in weddings. The duck represents true happiness and faithfulness among Chinese couples, and also matrimonial affection and trustworthiness between husband and wife.

See instructions for Nanuma Duck on page 129.

6" × 6" (15.2 × 15.2 cm)

Planet Venus
"Morning Star, Four Directions"

Also known as Morning Star, the Planet Venus symbol is commonly identified within astronomy. It has also been widely seen as a sculptured figure that appears as a glyph inscription within South America. The Mayans were one of the first cultures to adopt the Planet Venus. The Maya people identified this symbol as a planetary entity that made close connections with their rain god, Chaac.

This symbol was also linked to Kukulcan, the feathered serpent. It usually consists mainly of a bordered or outlined cross with four small circles around it. The four circles represent the four faces of Planet Venus, which is associated with the four different directions. The Maya people also associated Planet Venus with bright stars.

Planet Venus can have various representations such as a star with five points, a part of a face with two eyes, or half a star with a circle inside.

The Planet Venus symbol allows you the opportunity to make it the star that it is. Alternate the visual striped patterning by using a bright golden fabric. Use a glimmery, gold lamé as the alternate. Because lamé is manmade and can be very flimsy, back it with a lightweight fusible webbing to give the lamé body. Once the lamé is backed, you will be able to use it the same way that you use your quilt fabrics.

CULTURES

The Planet Venus symbol is also related to the people of Venezuela, who associate it with mythology. They identify it as a morning or evening star. More recently, modern astronomers identify Planet Venus solely as a planet.

Sumerian priests also recognize the Venus symbol as a planet, and have composed hymns using it as a theme.

CROSSING

See instructions for Planet Venus on page 132.

Four Stars

 Edward Bostick
enjoys founda-
tion piecing.
The Planet Venus symbol
reminds the quilt maker of
the string piecing patterns
that were created by African
American quilters indigenous
to the south. The women
sewed pieces of scraps, no
matter how small, to create
quilts that could be more
than queen-size. They used
fabrics left over from prior
sewing projects and old
clothing that could no longer
be worn. Bostick chose yellow
and white for the pattern to
show the rays of the planet,
a star radiating outward
from its center. The black
background represents the
never-ending universe where
the Planet Venus resides.

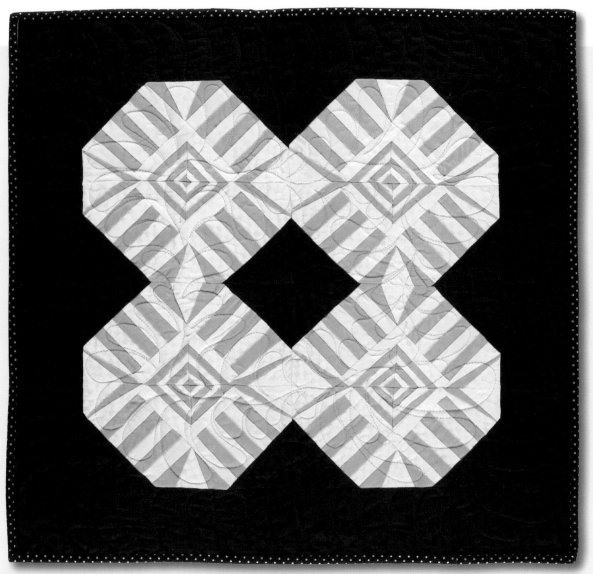

23½" × 23"
(59.7 × 58.4 cm)
2008
Edward Bostick

20" × 18"
(50.8 × 45.7 cm)
2006
Myrah Brown
Green &
Amenawon R.
Green

My daughter, Amenawon, and I created this quilt together. Amenawon made the foundation patterns, we shared the design concept, and I quilted it. This quilt is a call to women elders to mentor younger generations by imparting information that can benefit their future. Nanuma Duck, which symbolizes Mother Earth, represents the bearer of all wisdom. Although Nanuma is a South American symbol, Mother Earth is a universal one. The small duck that will one day become the leader follows the elder duck. The elder duck teaches the smaller duck the ways of the world—how to become a woman, a nurturing mother, and an upstanding citizen—so that it will know how to balance her daily life's rituals without losing her "self" in a world that is not of her nature.

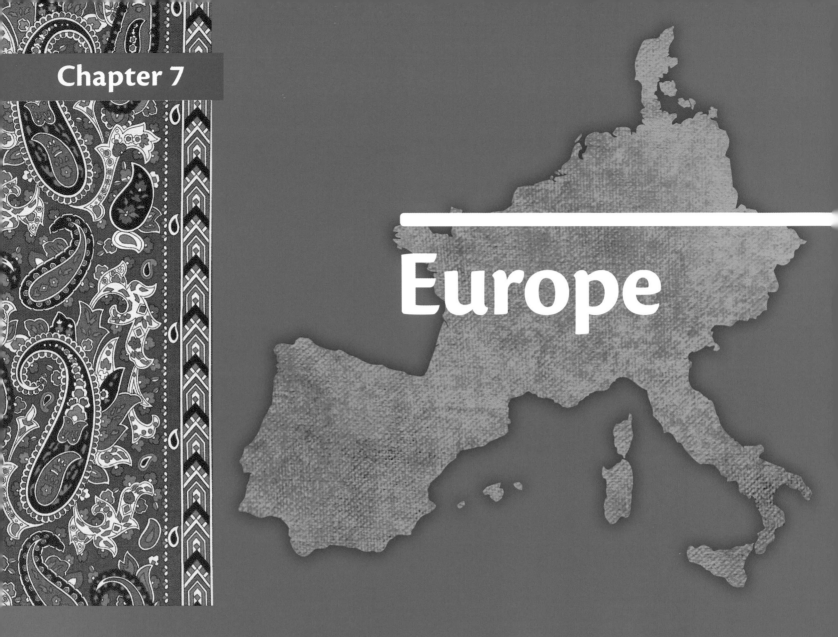

Chapter 7

Europe

Europe covers a variety of countries that each has its own culture. As early as the Paleolithic Period, a rich artistic culture emerged. The Greek word "paleo" translates to "old" and "lithos" means "stone." Sometime around 40,000 to 8,000 BCE, stone tools, weapons, and figures similar to the Goddess symbol represented in this chapter ignited Europe's artistic legacy.

Architecture, sculpture, and other forms of crafts all made their appearance during the Paleolithic Period. Sewing needles derived from bone and thread made from animal tendons were used to stitch hide into clothing. Art in Europe became more sophisticated between 28,000 and 10,000 BCE, when images were painted on cave walls in central and southern France and northern Spain.

Spirituality in art became a visual force in Europe during 500 CE. Early Medieval art was dominant, and Irish missionaries and Celtic monasteries were present. The book of Kells was one of the most popular medieval books of the time, known for its colorful monograms.

Celtic artists reaffirmed their heritage through the interlacing and spiral designs used to form the monograms.

Books played a very important part in the learning of European cultural practices and spiritual beliefs during this time, especially books of the gospels. Paintings of evangelists, angels, and other special figures were painted on the pages of these sacred books. Later, Greek, Romanesque, and Gothic art developed, reminding us how far the art of Europe has come since the Paleolithic Period.

During the 18th century, European scholars and others explored different parts of the world. These travelers brought back symbols and other forms of artistic treasures like obelisks and the fresco painting technique that originated in Egypt. West African masks indigenous to the royal court of Benin, created using the lost wax process, were brought back as well. Europe became one of the world's most diverse metropolitan continents, fusing together a variety of cultural symbols and artistic ideas.

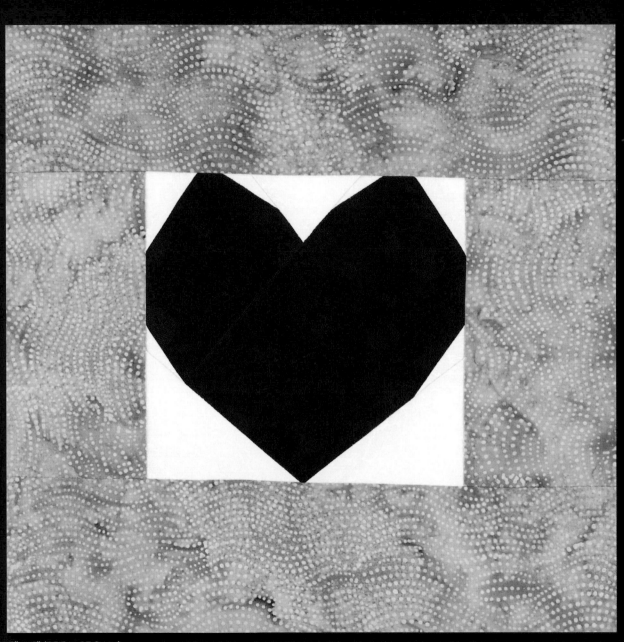

6" × 6" (15.2 × 15.2 cm)

Heart
"Love, Emotion"

The illustration of the traditional European Heart symbol vaguely represents the human heart, yet it has been used to symbolize love and affection since the 12th century. It is usually colored in red to symbolize blood, passion, and strong emotion. European scholars, including the Greek philosopher Aristotle, believed the heart to be the foundation of thought, reasoning, and passion, diminishing the brain's worth.

Since the 15th century, the Heart symbol has represented one of the red suits in a deck of playing cards. The shape of this symbol has been said to resemble the back and wings of a dove, associated with Aphrodite, the Greek goddess of love. Some also believe that the heart's shape also depicts features of a woman's body. However, the meaning of this iconic symbol is what matters more than its visual imagery.

CULTURES

In ancient Egyptian culture, the heart of the deceased was weighed against a feather when that person transcended. If the heart weighed more than the feather, it was determined that the individual was accepted into paradise.

CROSSING

See instructions
for Heart
on page 135.

3" × 6" (7.6 × 15.2 cm)

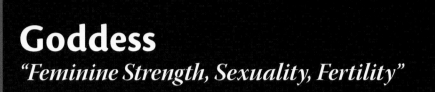

Goddess
"Feminine Strength, Sexuality, Fertility"

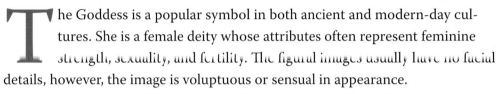

The Goddess is a popular symbol in both ancient and modern-day cultures. She is a female deity whose attributes often represent feminine strength, sexuality, and fertility. The figural images usually have no facial details, however, the image is voluptuous or sensual in appearance.

Every culture has a female deity or Goddess symbol. These Goddesses are usually part of a belief system in which several deities exist, including male deities or gods.

During the 19th century, a number of female figurines that were thought to exist since the Upper Paleolithic Period (35,000–25,000 BCE) were found in Europe. One of the most well known is the Venus of Willendorf, or the Great Goddess of Willendorf. Since so many were found, the figurines were disregarded as mere toys carved by men to satisfy their own sexual pleasures. The bodies conveyed exaggerated female attributes, including large breasts, a large stomach, wide hips, and thick thighs. It was not until a majority of these female images were found placed onto what appeared to be spiritual altars that scholars realized that the women had been elevated to divinity. Their bodies represented fertility and the strength to bear a child.

CULTURES

The deity of the Yoruba people of Nigeria, Yemaya, is an orisha spirit or goddess that symbolizes feminine strength, motherhood, and fertility. During childbirth, women called upon her to aid with a successful and safe delivery as early as 9th century CE. Today, when women have trouble conceiving, Yemaya is the goddess or deity to whom they pray.

CROSSING

See instructions
for Goddess
on page 137.

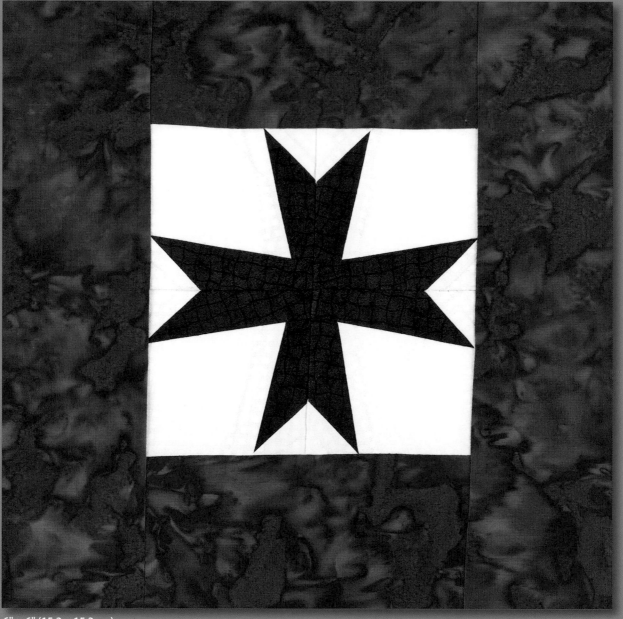

6" × 6" (15.2 × 15.2 cm)

Maltese Cross
"Courage, Protection, Direction"

The Maltese Cross was created in the early 11th century by Amalfian merchants who lived in a small Italian republic. It was a symbol of the Christian faith identifying those who moved out of the area known today as Malta, an island located in the Mediterranean Sea off the coast of North Africa and southern Europe. Around 1,070 CE, the Amalfian merchants founded the Knights of Malta, a Christian order of religious warriors. The purpose of the order was to protect those making the pilgrimage to the Holy Land.

The design of the cross has eight points, made up of four V-shaped arrow-like patterns. Each pattern meets at the center of the Maltese Cross symbol. The eight points of the cross represent the vows that the knights were to follow: truth, humility, faith, love of justice, mercy, sincerity, and endurance of persecution. The eight points also symbolize the eight points of courage, which include loyalty, holiness, honesty, bravery, glory and honor, contempt of death, helpfulness toward the poor and the sick, and respect for the church.

Although the Maltese Cross has been used by the Christian community over a number of years, it has been wrongly interpreted by the public as a symbol used by Hitler because it closely resembles the Iron Cross. Hitler used the cross with a superimposed swastika in the center as a symbol of prestige. At the end of World War II, the swastika was banned in Germany and around the world, prohibiting its use by all military and political organizations.

CULTURES CROSSING

The United States firefighter badge design is a variation of the Maltese Cross. The Knights of St. John, a courageous group of European crusaders, fought to save many of their fellow crusaders while in a fiery battle to protect the Holy Land. These men are considered the original firefighters. Today, the firefighter who is willing to wear the badge of the Maltese Cross is willing to sacrifice his or her life for a fellow firefighter just like the Knights of St. John did for their fellow crusaders.

See instructions for Maltese Cross on page 138.

Heart-Filled Memories

This piece was created to celebrate the gift of love. Quilt maker Dorothy Brown recalled all of her friends and family who have continued to shower her with love over the years as she pieced each heart. When reading about the heart, Brown learned that it is at the seat of emotion, mood, compassion, affection, and character. Because her emotions were uplifted while creating this quilt, she used a combination of bright, vivid fabrics to express her feelings. She echoed the heart shape inside of the large pink hearts with purple free-motion stitching. Although she was told that the Heart symbol is indigenous to Europe, Brown was drawn to machine quilt the Adinkra symbol in the small heart. It just seemed to fit perfectly in that space.

24¼" × 35"
(61.6 × 88.9 cm)
2007
Dorothy A. Brown

38" × 38½"
(96.5 × 97.8 cm)
2006
Ruth Marchese

All of the symbols Ruth Marchese assembled in "Hope 05" have special meaning to the quilt maker. They are very personal interpretations of world symbols, which spoke to her need of hope in a world that she perceives as careening toward self-destruction and despair. The Turtle is self-sufficient, able to shelter and protect himself; the Kanaga Crocodile takes advantage of every ray of sunshine; the Goddess is the essence of our existence; and the Eye of Heru watches over us. The dancing figures appliquéd on the quilt correspond to Marchese's need for a "lighter" world. With the colors red, green, and yellow, she tried to express hope for a better future.

Instructions

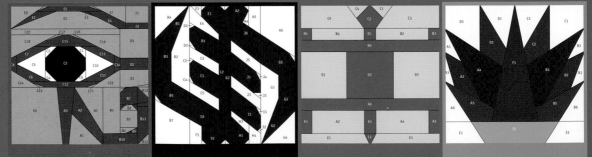

On the following pages you will find a pattern for each of the symbols featured throughout this book. Patterns have been provided in reverse, so you will simply need to photocopy the page and use with your desired fabrics. You'll also find step-by-step instructions for each section of the pattern, and finally assembly instructions to help you put together the various sections.

To make the process even simpler, pattern pieces are color coded to distinguish the use of different fabrics.

With access to so many different fabrics at your fingertips, choosing fabrics to complement your pieced symbols is easier than ever. Doing a little research on colors indigenous to the various continents will help you select the best fabrics. Adinkra symbols, like the Gye Nyame, for example, are usually stamped on a white, black, or saturated colored cotton cloth.

There are a number of faux reptile fabrics available in fabric stores and online. Because of today's modern technology, many of those fabrics have similar weights as the average 100-percent cotton quilting cloths. Step out of your comfort zone and use one of those reptile-like fabrics to re-create the body of the Rainbow Serpent, for example. Use a sequin or glass bead for the eye or use a dot of puff paint to bring this Aboriginal creature to life.

Once you've decided on your fabric, choosing embellishments can be a lot of fun. Charms, fringe, buttons, distinct stitching patterns, and more can add character to your pieced symbols and also reflect the continent from which the symbol reigns. Stitching curvy lines coming out of the Kokopelli's flute to give the appearance of music or sound, for example, can enhance the look of the symbol.

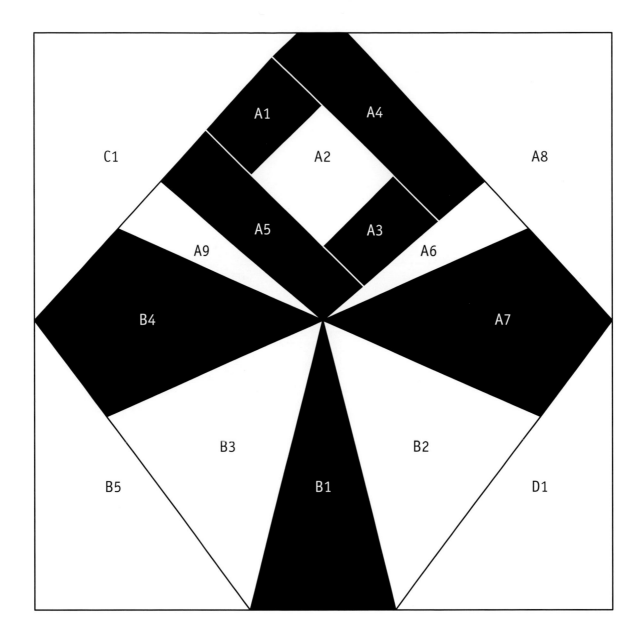

See the block and
story of Ankh
on page 18.

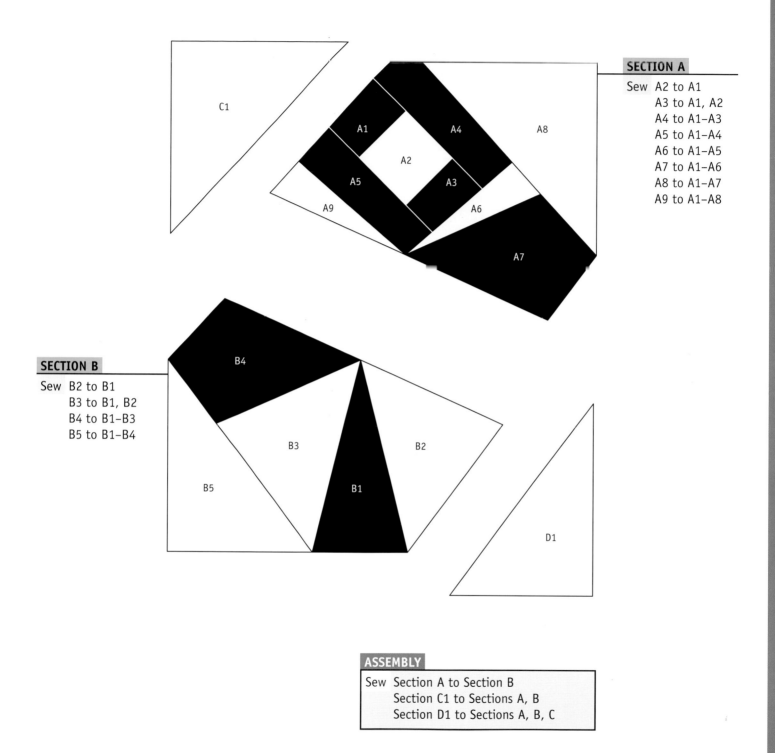

C1

SECTION A

A1
A2
A3
A4
A5
A6
A7
A8
A9

Sew A2 to A1
A3 to A1, A2
A4 to A1–A3
A5 to A1–A4
A6 to A1–A5
A7 to A1–A6
A8 to A1–A7
A9 to A1–A8

SECTION B

Sew B2 to B1
B3 to B1, B2
B4 to B1–B3
B5 to B1–B4

B1
B2
B3
B4
B5

D1

ASSEMBLY

Sew Section A to Section B
Section C1 to Sections A, B
Section D1 to Sections A, B, C

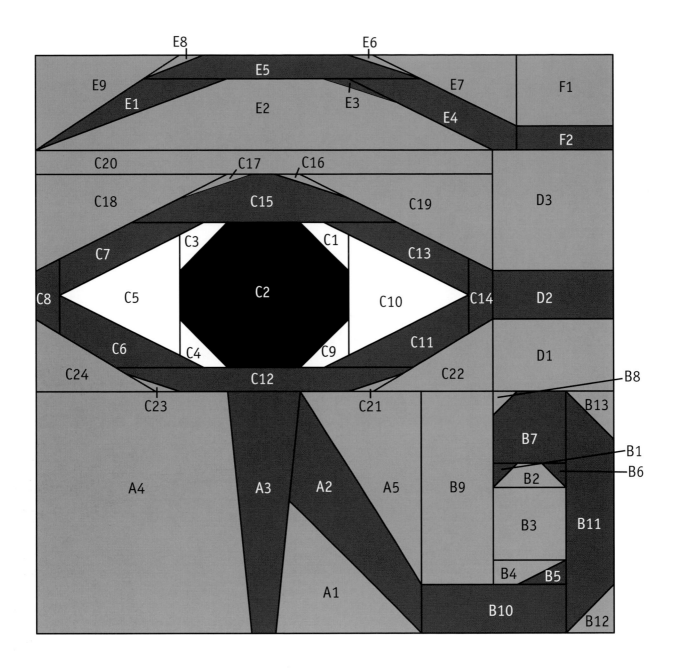

See the block and
story of Eye of Heru
on page 20.

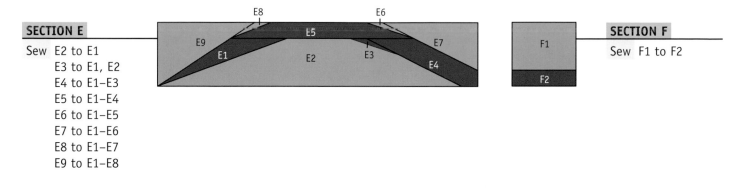

SECTION E

Sew E2 to E1
E3 to E1, E2
E4 to E1–E3
E5 to E1–E4
E6 to E1–E5
E7 to E1–E6
E8 to E1–E7
E9 to E1–E8

SECTION F

Sew F1 to F2

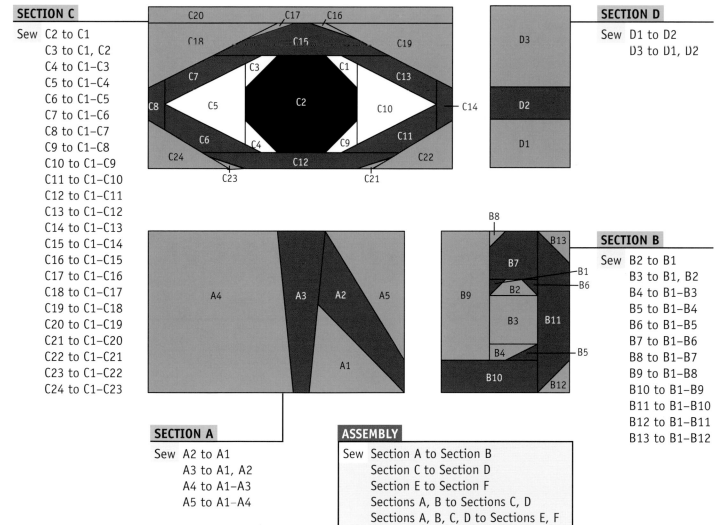

SECTION C

Sew C2 to C1
C3 to C1, C2
C4 to C1–C3
C5 to C1–C4
C6 to C1–C5
C7 to C1–C6
C8 to C1–C7
C9 to C1–C8
C10 to C1–C9
C11 to C1–C10
C12 to C1–C11
C13 to C1–C12
C14 to C1–C13
C15 to C1–C14
C16 to C1–C15
C17 to C1–C16
C18 to C1–C17
C19 to C1–C18
C20 to C1–C19
C21 to C1–C20
C22 to C1–C21
C23 to C1–C22
C24 to C1–C23

SECTION D

Sew D1 to D2
D3 to D1, D2

SECTION B

Sew B2 to B1
B3 to B1, B2
B4 to B1–B3
B5 to B1–B4
B6 to B1–B5
B7 to B1–B6
B8 to B1–B7
B9 to B1–B8
B10 to B1–B9
B11 to B1–B10
B12 to B1–B11
B13 to B1–B12

SECTION A

Sew A2 to A1
A3 to A1, A2
A4 to A1–A3
A5 to A1–A4

ASSEMBLY

Sew Section A to Section B
Section C to Section D
Section E to Section F
Sections A, B to Sections C, D
Sections A, B, C, D to Sections E, F

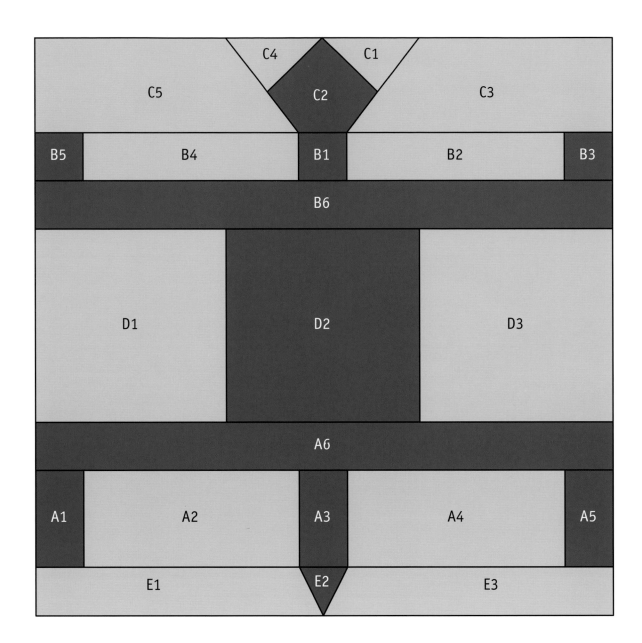

See the block and story
of Kanaga Crocodile
on page 22.

SECTION C

Sew C2 to C1
C3 to C1, C2
C4 to C1–C3
C5 to C1–C4

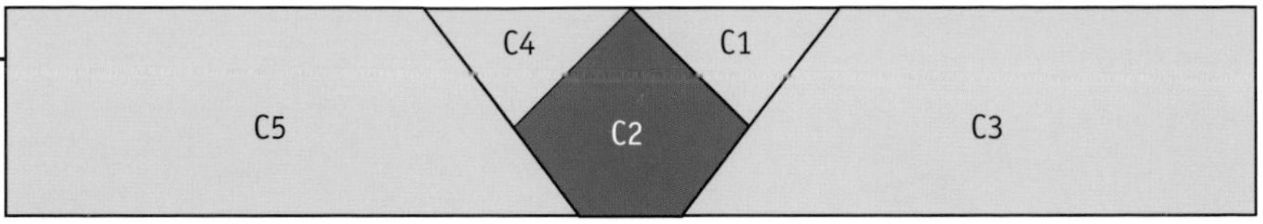

C4	C1	
C5	C2	C3

SECTION B

Sew B2 to B1
B3 to B1, B2
B4 to B1–B3
B5 to B1–B4
B6 to B1–B5

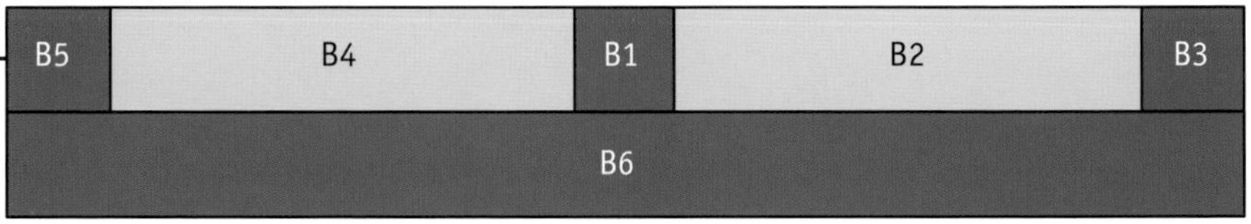

B5	B4	B1	B2	B3
B6				

SECTION D

Sew D2 to D1
D3 to D1, D2

D1	D2	D3

SECTION A

Sew A2 to A1
A3 to A1, A2
A4 to A1–A3
A5 to A1–A4
A6 to A1–A5

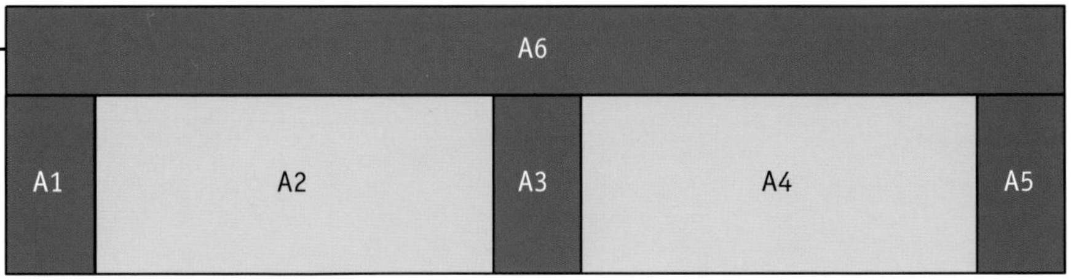

A6				
A1	A2	A3	A4	A5

SECTION E

Sew E2 to E1
E3 to E1, E2

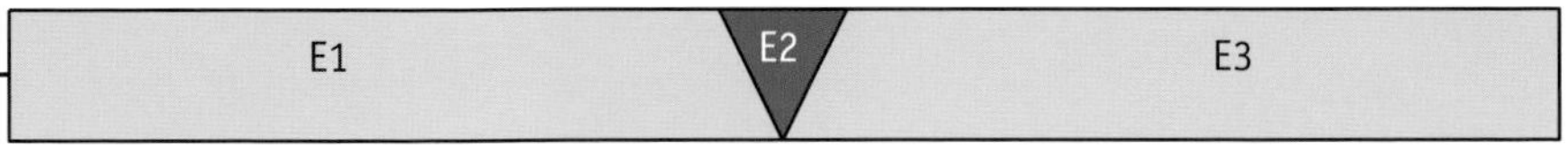

E1	E2	E3

ASSEMBLY

Sew Section A to Section E
Sections A, E to Section D
Sections A, E, D to Section B
Sections A, E, D, B to Section C

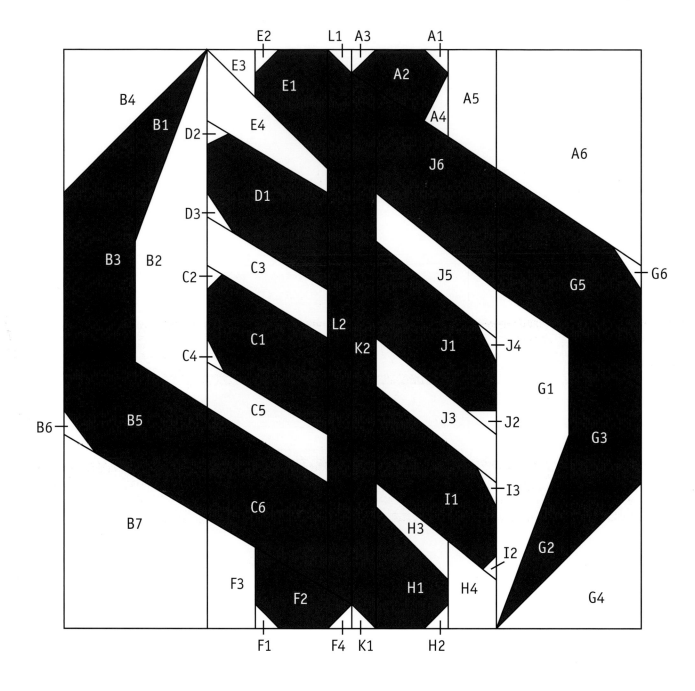

See the block and
story of Gye Nyame
on page 24.

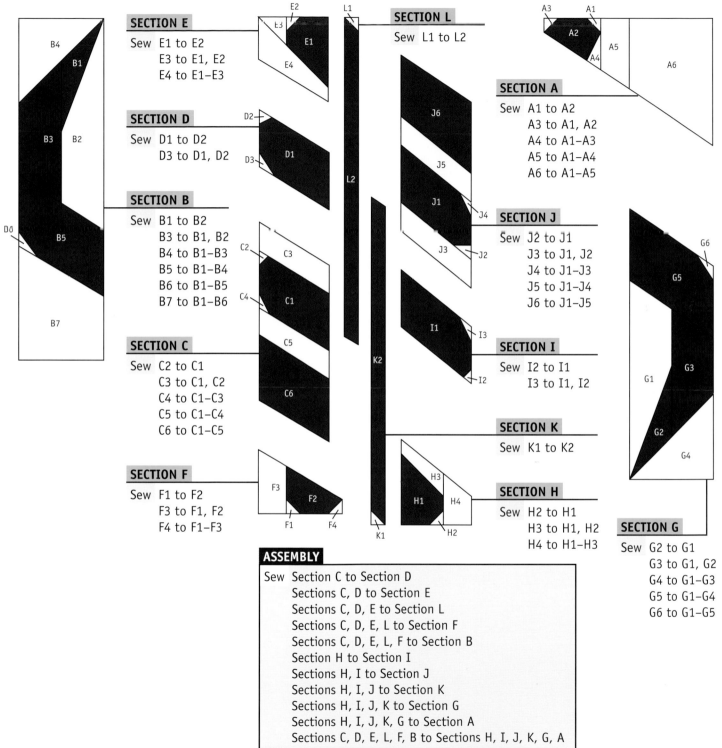

SECTION E

Sew E1 to E2
E3 to E1, E2
E4 to E1–E3

SECTION D

Sew D1 to D2
D3 to D1, D2

SECTION B

Sew B1 to B2
B3 to B1, B2
B4 to B1–B3
B5 to B1–B4
B6 to B1–B5
B7 to B1–B6

SECTION C

Sew C2 to C1
C3 to C1, C2
C4 to C1–C3
C5 to C1–C4
C6 to C1–C5

SECTION F

Sew F1 to F2
F3 to F1, F2
F4 to F1–F3

SECTION L

Sew L1 to L2

SECTION A

Sew A1 to A2
A3 to A1, A2
A4 to A1–A3
A5 to A1–A4
A6 to A1–A5

SECTION J

Sew J2 to J1
J3 to J1, J2
J4 to J1–J3
J5 to J1–J4
J6 to J1–J5

SECTION I

Sew I2 to I1
I3 to I1, I2

SECTION K

Sew K1 to K2

SECTION H

Sew H2 to H1
H3 to H1, H2
H4 to H1–H3

SECTION G

Sew G2 to G1
G3 to G1, G2
G4 to G1–G3
G5 to G1–G4
G6 to G1–G5

ASSEMBLY

Sew Section C to Section D
Sections C, D to Section E
Sections C, D, E to Section L
Sections C, D, E, L to Section F
Sections C, D, E, L, F to Section B
Section H to Section I
Sections H, I to Section J
Sections H, I, J to Section K
Sections H, I, J, K to Section G
Sections H, I, J, K, G to Section A
Sections C, D, E, L, F, B to Sections H, I, J, K, G, A

93

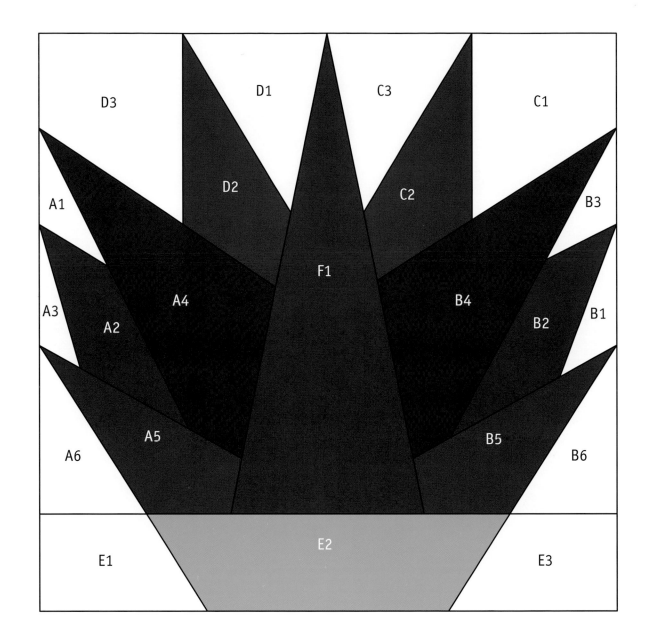

See the block and
story of Lotus Flower
on page 26.

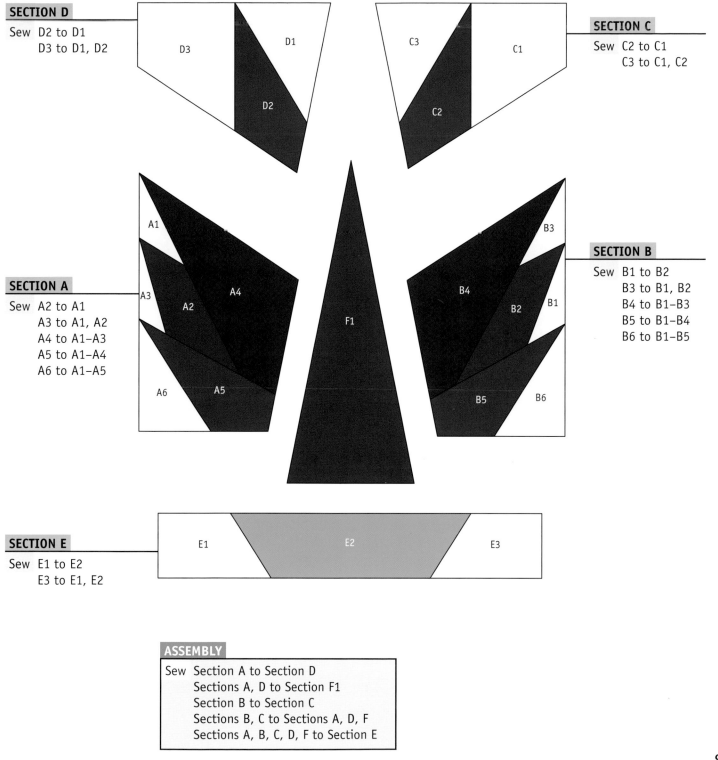

SECTION D

Sew D2 to D1
       D3 to D1, D2

SECTION C

Sew C2 to C1
       C3 to C1, C2

SECTION A

Sew A2 to A1
       A3 to A1, A2
       A4 to A1–A3
       A5 to A1–A4
       A6 to A1–A5

SECTION B

Sew B1 to B2
       B3 to B1, B2
       B4 to B1–B3
       B5 to B1–B4
       B6 to B1–B5

SECTION E

Sew E1 to E2
       E3 to E1, E2

ASSEMBLY

Sew Section A to Section D
       Sections A, D to Section F1
       Section B to Section C
       Sections B, C to Sections A, D, F
       Sections A, B, C, D, F to Section E

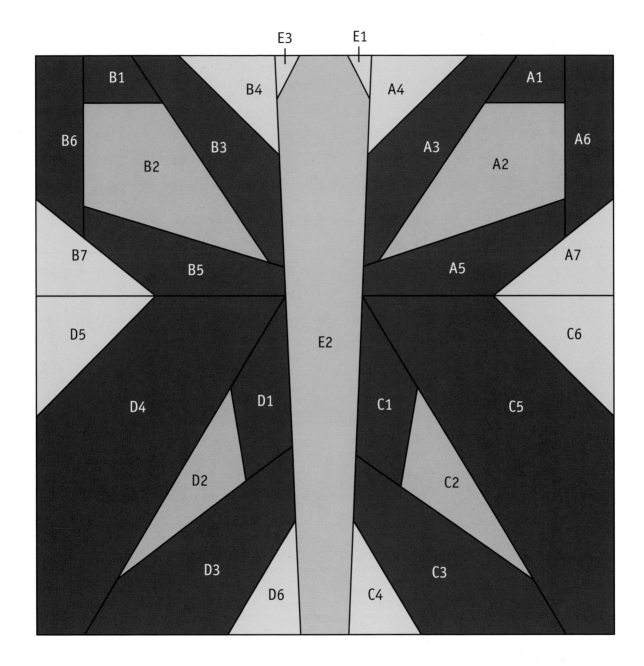

See the block and
story of Butterfly
on page 32.

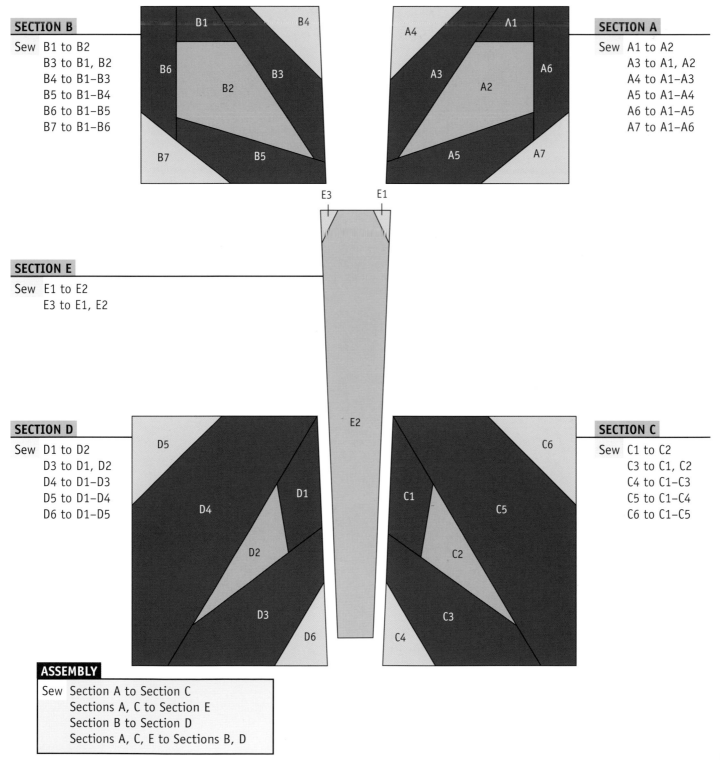

SECTION B

Sew B1 to B2
B3 to B1, B2
B4 to B1–B3
B5 to B1–B4
B6 to B1–B5
B7 to B1–B6

SECTION A

Sew A1 to A2
A3 to A1, A2
A4 to A1–A3
A5 to A1–A4
A6 to A1–A5
A7 to A1–A6

SECTION E

Sew E1 to E2
E3 to E1, E2

SECTION D

Sew D1 to D2
D3 to D1, D2
D4 to D1–D3
D5 to D1–D4
D6 to D1–D5

SECTION C

Sew C1 to C2
C3 to C1, C2
C4 to C1–C3
C5 to C1–C4
C6 to C1–C5

ASSEMBLY

Sew Section A to Section C
Sections A, C to Section E
Section B to Section D
Sections A, C, E to Sections B, D

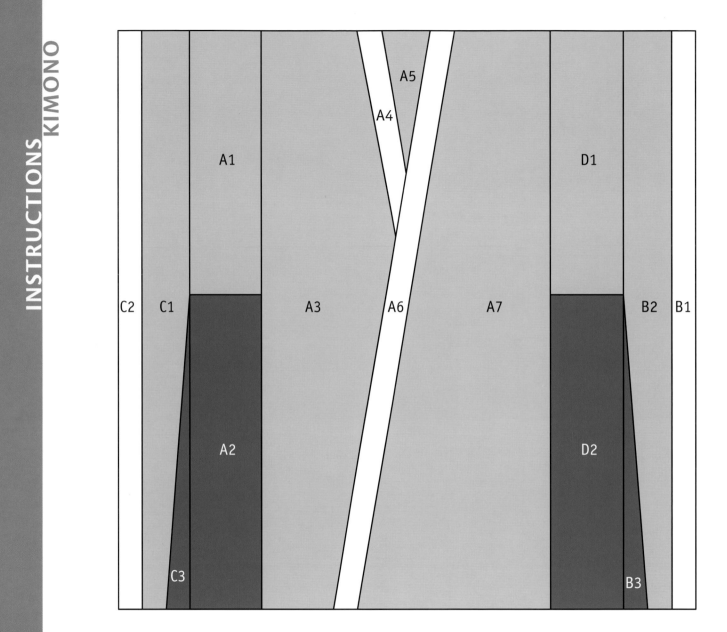

See the block and
story of Kimono
on page 34.

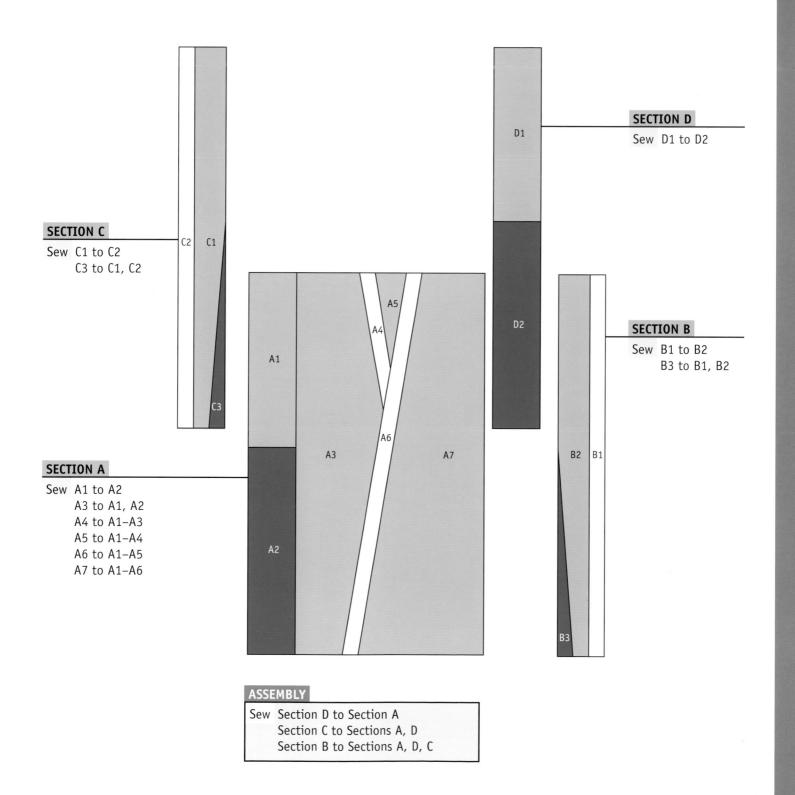

SECTION C

Sew C1 to C2
      C3 to C1, C2

SECTION A

Sew A1 to A2
      A3 to A1, A2
      A4 to A1–A3
      A5 to A1–A4
      A6 to A1–A5
      A7 to A1–A6

SECTION D

Sew D1 to D2

SECTION B

Sew B1 to B2
      B3 to B1, B2

ASSEMBLY

Sew Section D to Section A
      Section C to Sections A, D
      Section B to Sections A, D, C

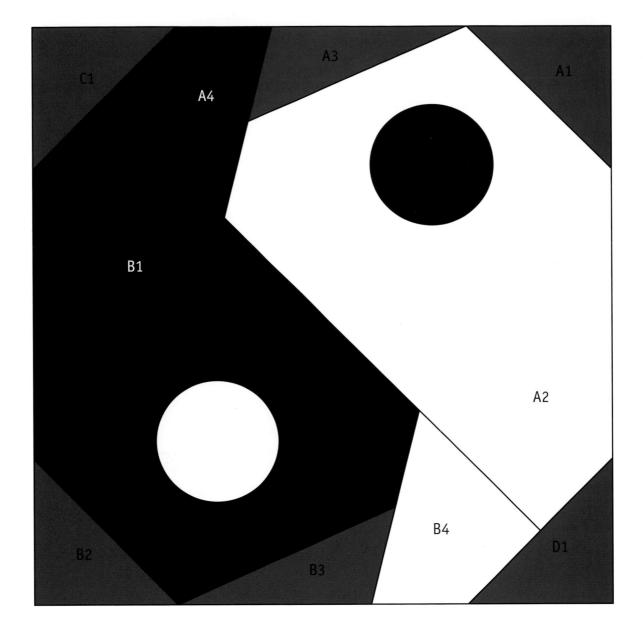

See the block and
story of Yin & Yang
on page 36.

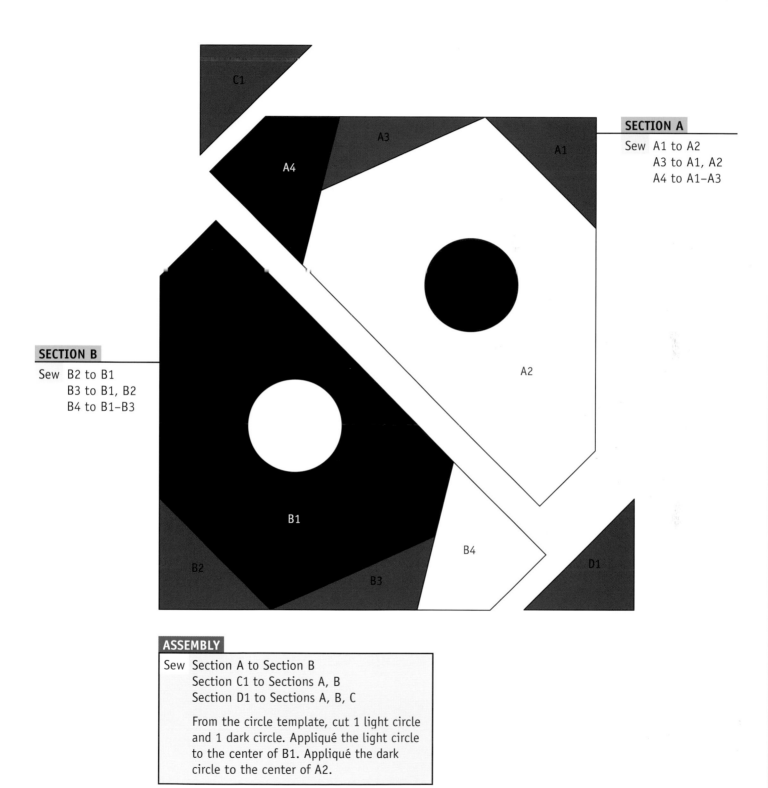

C1

A3

A4

A1

SECTION A

Sew A1 to A2
     A3 to A1, A2
     A4 to A1–A3

A2

SECTION B

Sew B2 to B1
     B3 to B1, B2
     B4 to B1–B3

B1

B2

B4

B3

D1

ASSEMBLY

Sew Section A to Section B
     Section C1 to Sections A, B
     Section D1 to Sections A, B, C

     From the circle template, cut 1 light circle
     and 1 dark circle. Appliqué the light circle
     to the center of B1. Appliqué the dark
     circle to the center of A2.

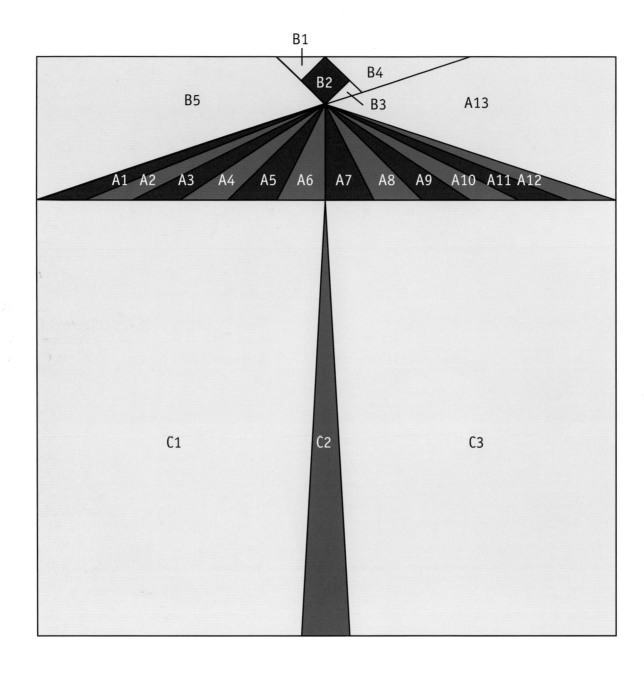

See the block and
story of Parasol
on page 38.

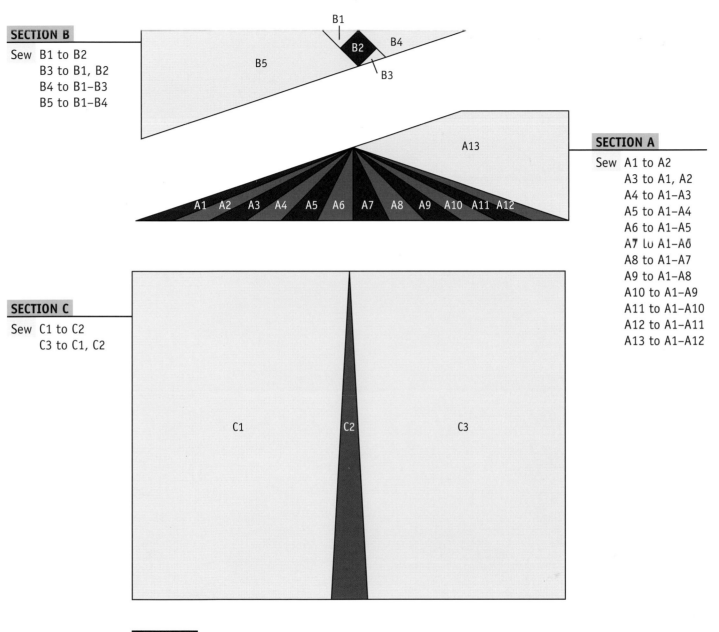

SECTION B

Sew B1 to B2
     B3 to B1, B2
     B4 to B1–B3
     B5 to B1–B4

B1
B2
B4
B5
B3

SECTION A

Sew A1 to A2
     A3 to A1, A2
     A4 to A1–A3
     A5 to A1–A4
     A6 to A1–A5
     A7 to A1–A6
     A8 to A1–A7
     A9 to A1–A8
     A10 to A1–A9
     A11 to A1–A10
     A12 to A1–A11
     A13 to A1–A12

A13

A1 A2 A3 A4 A5 A6 A7 A8 A9 A10 A11 A12

SECTION C

Sew C1 to C2
     C3 to C1, C2

C1   C2   C3

ASSEMBLY

Sew Section A to Section B
     Sections A, B to Section C

103

TOP

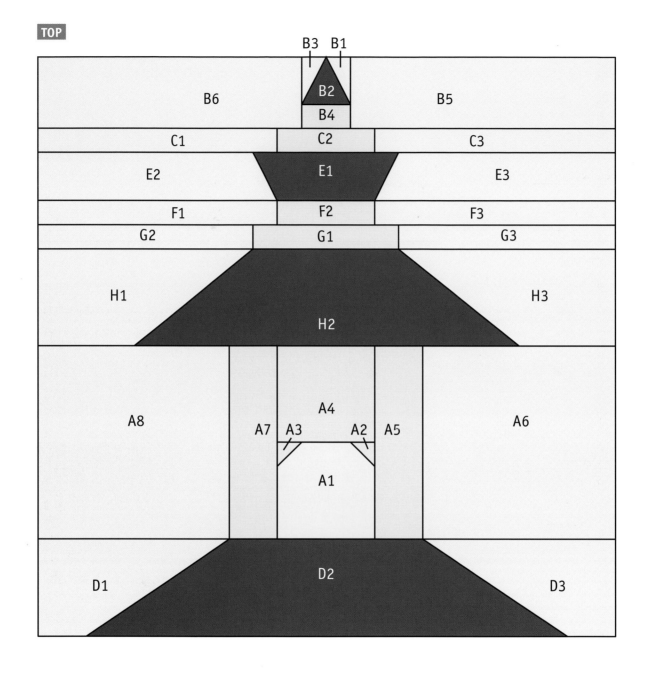

See the block and
story of Pagoda
on page 40.

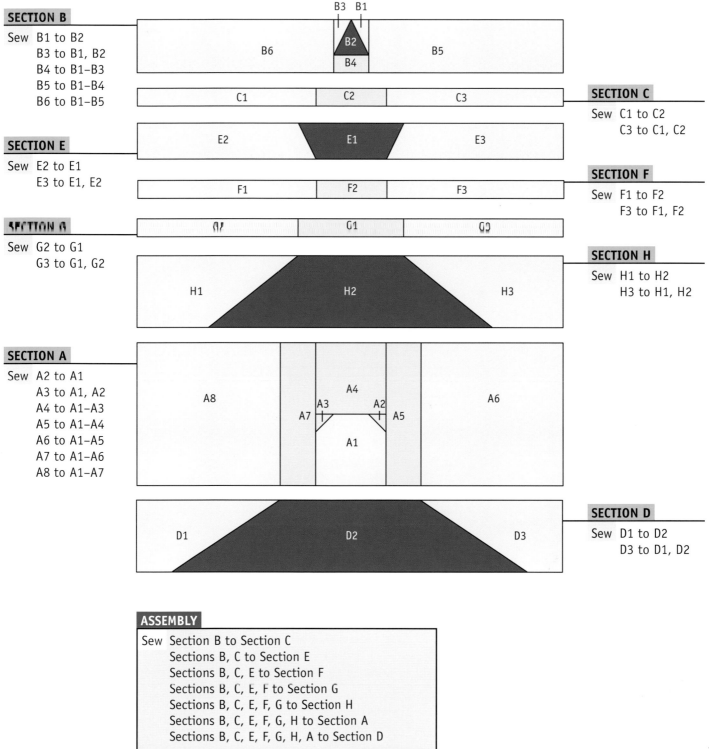

SECTION B

Sew B1 to B2
B3 to B1, B2
B4 to B1–B3
B5 to B1–B4
B6 to B1–B5

SECTION C

Sew C1 to C2
C3 to C1, C2

SECTION E

Sew E2 to E1
E3 to E1, E2

SECTION F

Sew F1 to F2
F3 to F1, F2

SECTION G

Sew G2 to G1
G3 to G1, G2

SECTION H

Sew H1 to H2
H3 to H1, H2

SECTION A

Sew A2 to A1
A3 to A1, A2
A4 to A1–A3
A5 to A1–A4
A6 to A1–A5
A7 to A1–A6
A8 to A1–A7

SECTION D

Sew D1 to D2
D3 to D1, D2

ASSEMBLY

Sew Section B to Section C
Sections B, C to Section E
Sections B, C, E to Section F
Sections B, C, E, F to Section G
Sections B, C, E, F, G to Section H
Sections B, C, E, F, G, H to Section A
Sections B, C, E, F, G, H, A to Section D

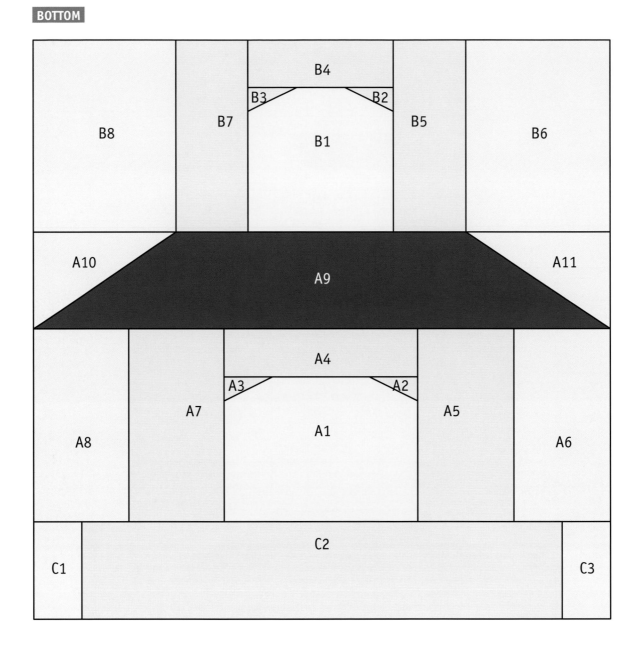

BOTTOM

B4
B3
B2
B8
B7
B1
B5
B6

A10
A9
A11

A4
A3
A2
A7
A5
A8
A1
A6

C2
C1
C3

See the block and
story of Pagoda
on page 40.

SECTION B

Sew B1 to B2
     B3 to B1, B2
     B4 to B1–B3
     B5 to B1–B4
     B6 to B1–B5
     B7 to B1–B6
     B8 to B1–B7

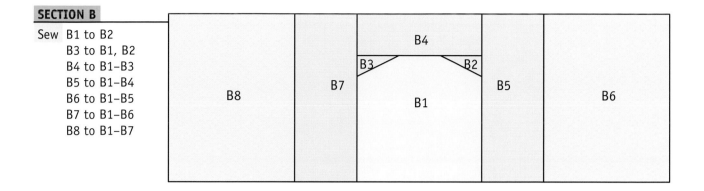

SECTION A

Sew A1 to A2
     A3 to A1, A2
     A4 to A1–A3
     A5 to A1–A4
     A6 to A1–A5
     A7 to A1–A6
     A8 to A1–A7
     A9 to A1–A8
     A10 to A1–A9
     A11 to A1–A10

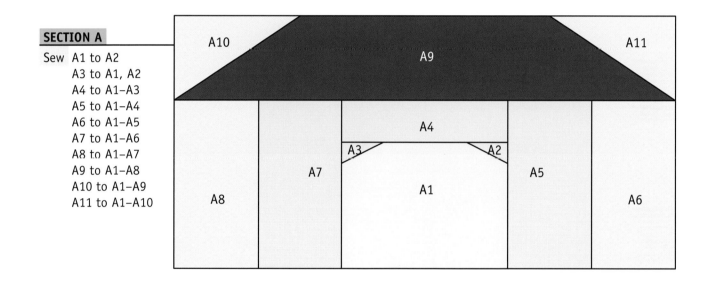

SECTION C

Sew C1 to C2
     C3 to C1, C2

ASSEMBLY

Sew Section B to Section A
     Sections B, A to Section C

     Sew top piece to bottom piece.

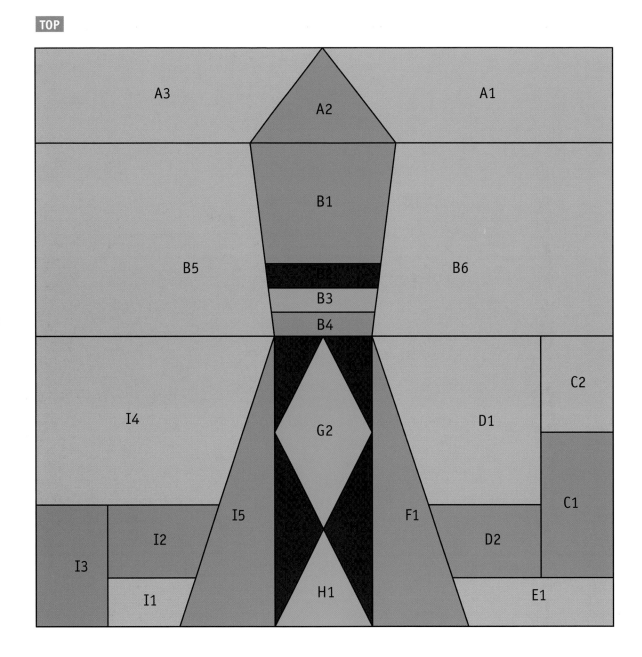

TOP

A3

A2

A1

B1

B5

B2

B3

B6

B4

I4

C2

G2

D1

I5

F1

C1

I2

D2

I3

I1

H1

E1

See the block and
story of Sacred
Totem on page 46.

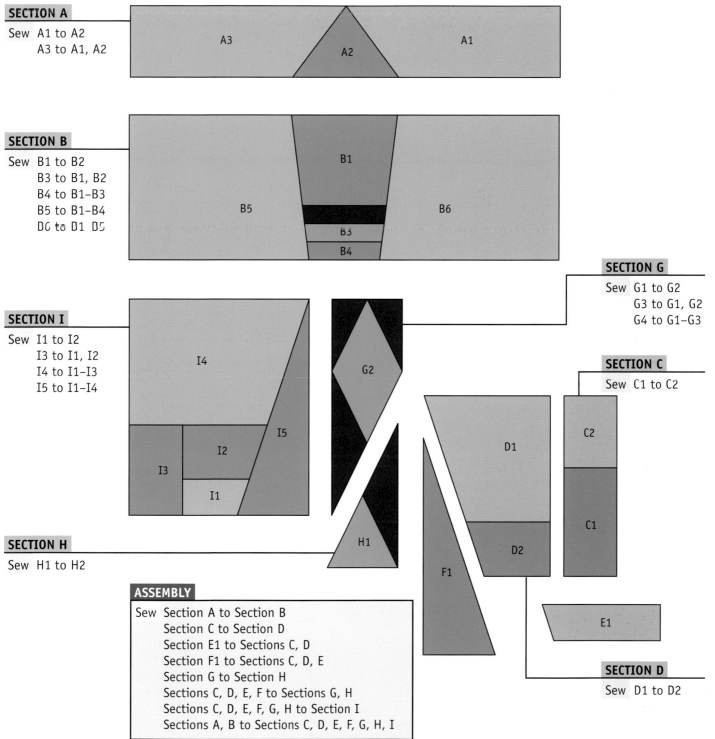

SECTION A

Sew A1 to A2
     A3 to A1, A2

SECTION B

Sew B1 to B2
     B3 to B1, B2
     B4 to B1–B3
     B5 to B1–B4
     D6 to D1–D5

A3

A2

A1

B1

B5

B6

B3

B4

SECTION G

Sew G1 to G2
     G3 to G1, G2
     G4 to G1–G3

SECTION I

Sew I1 to I2
     I3 to I1, I2
     I4 to I1–I3
     I5 to I1–I4

I4

I2

I3

I1

I5

G2

SECTION C

Sew C1 to C2

C2

C1

D1

D2

F1

E1

SECTION H

Sew H1 to H2

H1

ASSEMBLY

Sew Section A to Section B
     Section C to Section D
     Section E1 to Sections C, D
     Section F1 to Sections C, D, E
     Section G to Section H
     Sections C, D, E, F to Sections G, H
     Sections C, D, E, F, G, H to Section I
     Sections A, B to Sections C, D, E, F, G, H, I

SECTION D

Sew D1 to D2

MIDDLE

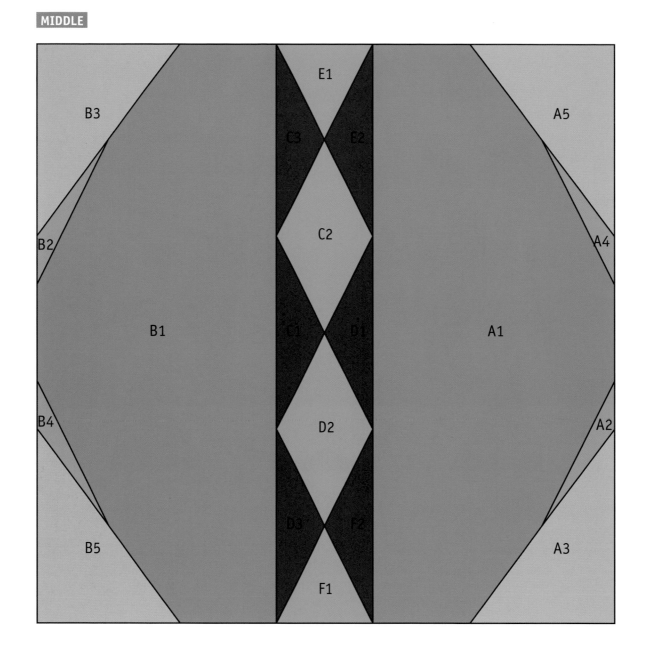

See the block and
story of Sacred
Totem on page 46.

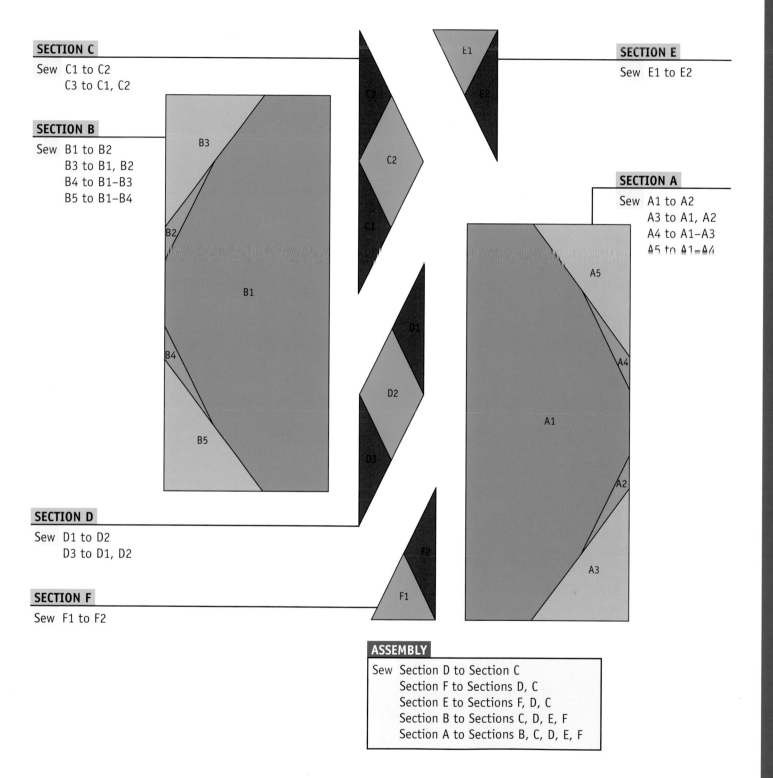

SECTION C

Sew C1 to C2
      C3 to C1, C2

SECTION B

Sew B1 to B2
      B3 to B1, B2
      B4 to B1–B3
      B5 to B1–B4

SECTION E

Sew E1 to E2

SECTION A

Sew A1 to A2
      A3 to A1, A2
      A4 to A1–A3
      A5 to A1–A4

SECTION D

Sew D1 to D2
      D3 to D1, D2

SECTION F

Sew F1 to F2

ASSEMBLY

Sew Section D to Section C
      Section F to Sections D, C
      Section E to Sections F, D, C
      Section B to Sections C, D, E, F
      Section A to Sections B, C, D, E, F

BOTTOM

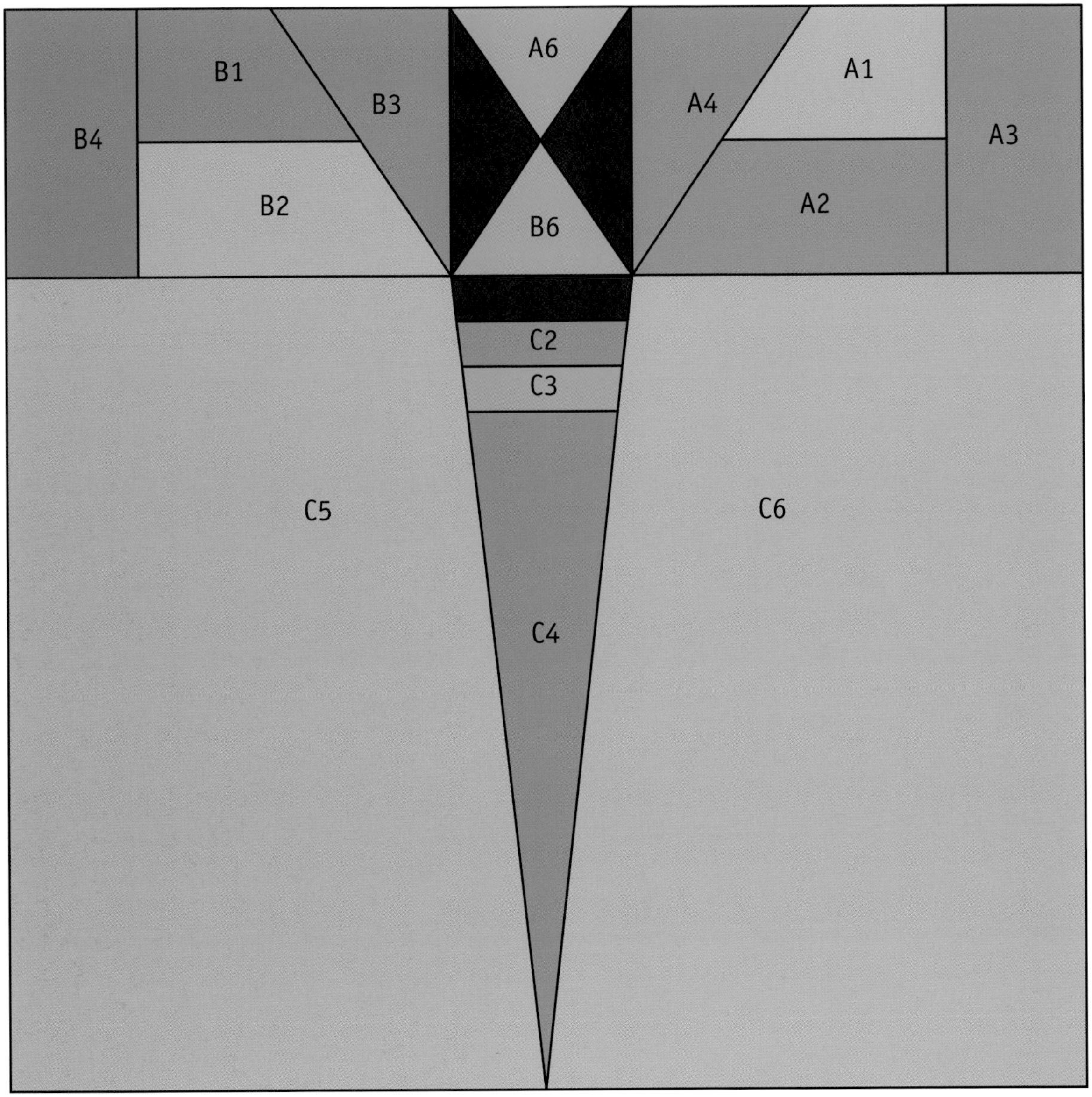

B4

B1

B3

A6

A4

A1

A3

B2

B6

A2

C2

C3

C5

C6

C4

See the block and
story of Sacred
Totem on page 46.

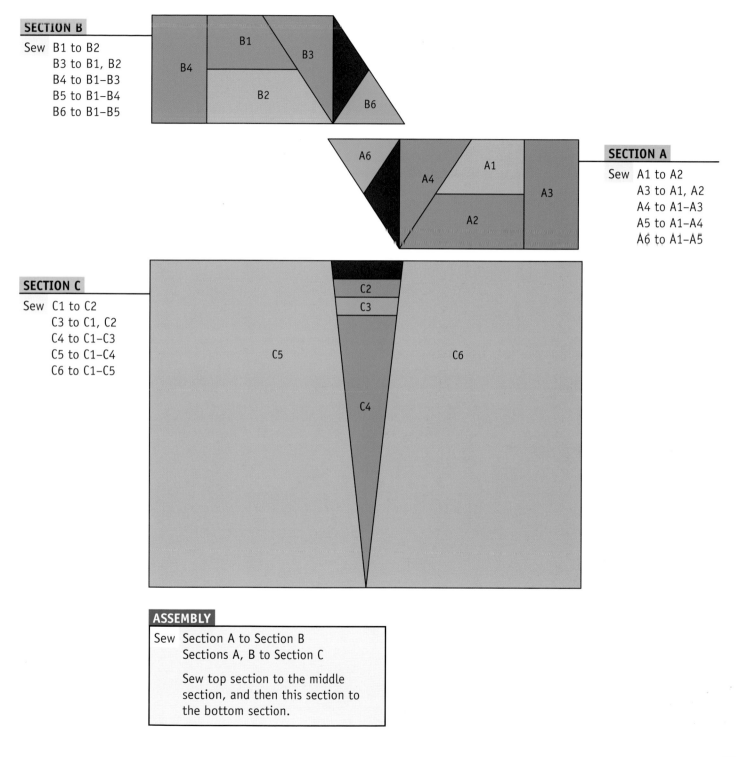

SECTION B

Sew B1 to B2
B3 to B1, B2
B4 to B1–B3
B5 to B1–B4
B6 to B1–B5

SECTION A

Sew A1 to A2
A3 to A1, A2
A4 to A1–A3
A5 to A1–A4
A6 to A1–A5

SECTION C

Sew C1 to C2
C3 to C1, C2
C4 to C1–C3
C5 to C1–C4
C6 to C1–C5

ASSEMBLY

Sew Section A to Section B
Sections A, B to Section C

Sew top section to the middle section, and then this section to the bottom section.

113

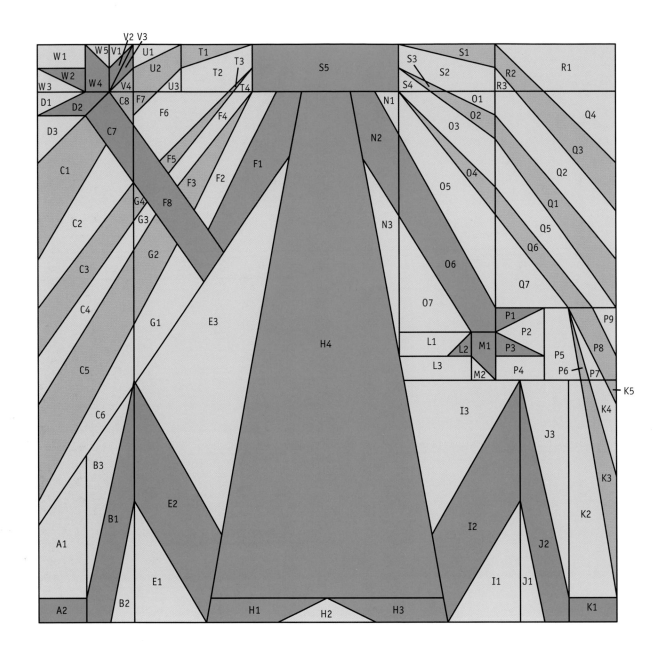

See the block and story of
Lightning Spirit Ancestor
on page 48.

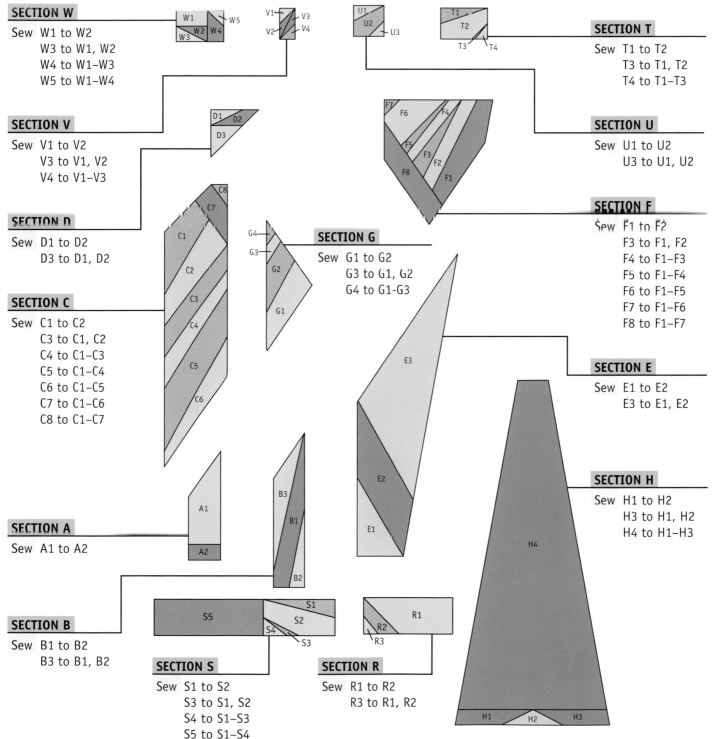

SECTION W

Sew W1 to W2
W3 to W1, W2
W4 to W1–W3
W5 to W1–W4

SECTION V

Sew V1 to V2
V3 to V1, V2
V4 to V1–V3

SECTION D

Sew D1 to D2
D3 to D1, D2

SECTION C

Sew C1 to C2
C3 to C1, C2
C4 to C1–C3
C5 to C1–C4
C6 to C1–C5
C7 to C1–C6
C8 to C1–C7

SECTION A

Sew A1 to A2

SECTION B

Sew B1 to B2
B3 to B1, B2

SECTION S

Sew S1 to S2
S3 to S1, S2
S4 to S1–S3
S5 to S1–S4

SECTION R

Sew R1 to R2
R3 to R1, R2

SECTION G

Sew G1 to G2
G3 to G1, G2
G4 to G1-G3

SECTION T

Sew T1 to T2
T3 to T1, T2
T4 to T1–T3

SECTION U

Sew U1 to U2
U3 to U1, U2

SECTION F

Sew F1 to F2
F3 to F1, F2
F4 to F1–F3
F5 to F1–F4
F6 to F1–F5
F7 to F1–F6
F8 to F1–F7

SECTION E

Sew E1 to E2
E3 to E1, E2

SECTION H

Sew H1 to H2
H3 to H1, H2
H4 to H1–H3

115

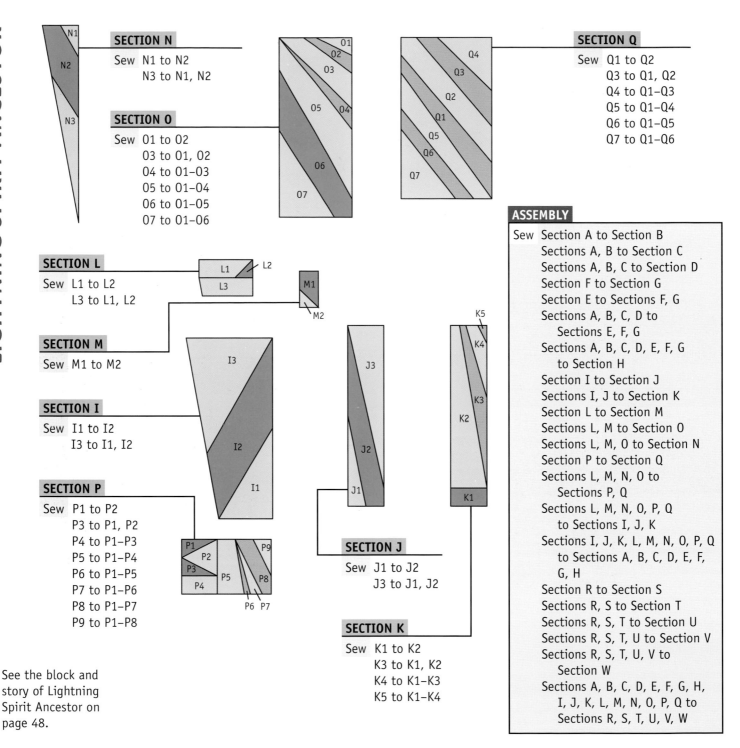

SECTION N

Sew N1 to N2
N3 to N1, N2

SECTION O

Sew O1 to O2
O3 to O1, O2
O4 to O1–O3
O5 to O1–O4
O6 to O1–O5
O7 to O1–O6

SECTION Q

Sew Q1 to Q2
Q3 to Q1, Q2
Q4 to Q1–Q3
Q5 to Q1–Q4
Q6 to Q1–Q5
Q7 to Q1–Q6

SECTION L

Sew L1 to L2
L3 to L1, L2

SECTION M

Sew M1 to M2

SECTION I

Sew I1 to I2
I3 to I1, I2

SECTION P

Sew P1 to P2
P3 to P1, P2
P4 to P1–P3
P5 to P1–P4
P6 to P1–P5
P7 to P1–P6
P8 to P1–P7
P9 to P1–P8

SECTION J

Sew J1 to J2
J3 to J1, J2

SECTION K

Sew K1 to K2
K3 to K1, K2
K4 to K1–K3
K5 to K1–K4

See the block and
story of Lightning
Spirit Ancestor on
page 48.

ASSEMBLY

Sew Section A to Section B
Sections A, B to Section C
Sections A, B, C to Section D
Section F to Section G
Section E to Sections F, G
Sections A, B, C, D to
Sections E, F, G
Sections A, B, C, D, E, F, G
to Section H
Section I to Section J
Sections I, J to Section K
Section L to Section M
Sections L, M to Section O
Sections L, M, O to Section N
Section P to Section Q
Sections L, M, N, O to
Sections P, Q
Sections L, M, N, O, P, Q
to Sections I, J, K
Sections I, J, K, L, M, N, O, P, Q
to Sections A, B, C, D, E, F,
G, H
Section R to Section S
Sections R, S to Section T
Sections R, S, T to Section U
Sections R, S, T, U to Section V
Sections R, S, T, U, V to
Section W
Sections A, B, C, D, E, F, G, H,
I, J, K, L, M, N, O, P, Q to
Sections R, S, T, U, V, W

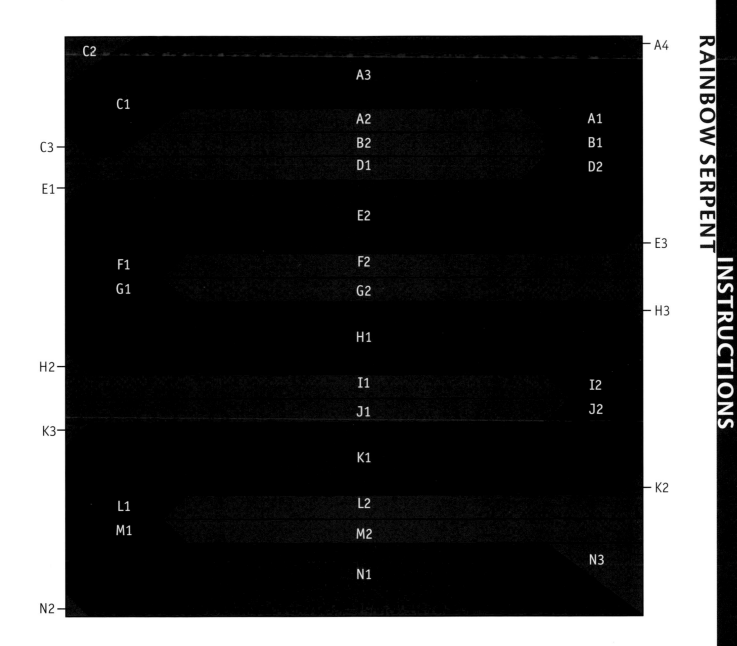

See the block and story
of Rainbow Serpent
on page 50.

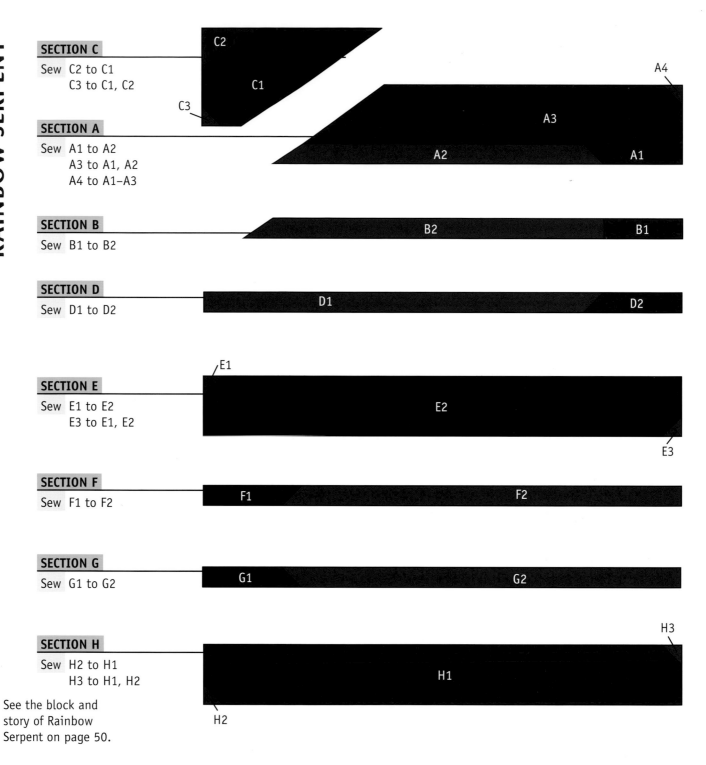

SECTION C

Sew   C2 to C1
      C3 to C1, C2

SECTION A

Sew   A1 to A2
      A3 to A1, A2
      A4 to A1–A3

SECTION B

Sew   B1 to B2

SECTION D

Sew   D1 to D2

SECTION E

Sew   E1 to E2
      E3 to E1, E2

SECTION F

Sew   F1 to F2

SECTION G

Sew   G1 to G2

SECTION H

Sew   H2 to H1
      H3 to H1, H2

See the block and
story of Rainbow
Serpent on page 50.

SECTION I

Sew I1 to I2

I1 ··· I2

SECTION J

Sew J2 to J1

J1 ··· J2

K3

SECTION K

Sew K2 to K1
     K3 to K1, K2

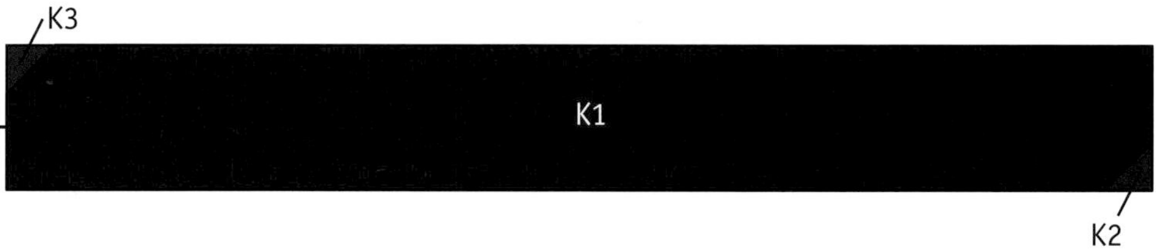

K1

K2

SECTION L

Sew L2 to L1

L1 ··· L2

SECTION M

Sew M2 to M1

M1 ··· M2

SECTION N

Sew N2 to N1
     N3 to N1, N2

N1 ··· N3

N2

ASSEMBLY

Sew Section A to Section B
     Section C to Sections A, B
     Section D to Sections A, B, C
     Section E to Sections A, B, C, D
     Section F to Sections A, B, C, D, E
     Section G to Sections A, B, C, D, E, F
     Section H to Sections A, B, C, D, E, F, G
     Section I to Sections A, B, C, D, E, F, G, H
     Section J to Sections A, B, C, D, E, F, G, H, I
     Section K to Sections A, B, C, D, E, F, G, H, I, J
     Section L to Sections A, B, C, D, E, F, G, H, I, J, K
     Section M to Sections A, B, C, D, E, F, G, H, I, J, K, L
     Section N to Sections A, B, C, D, E, F, G, H, I, J, K, L, M

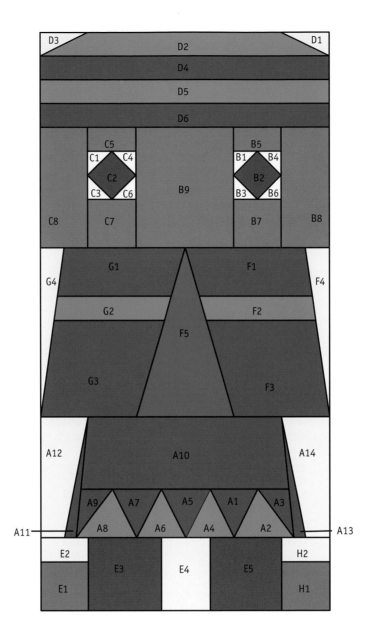

See the block and story of Kachina on page 56.

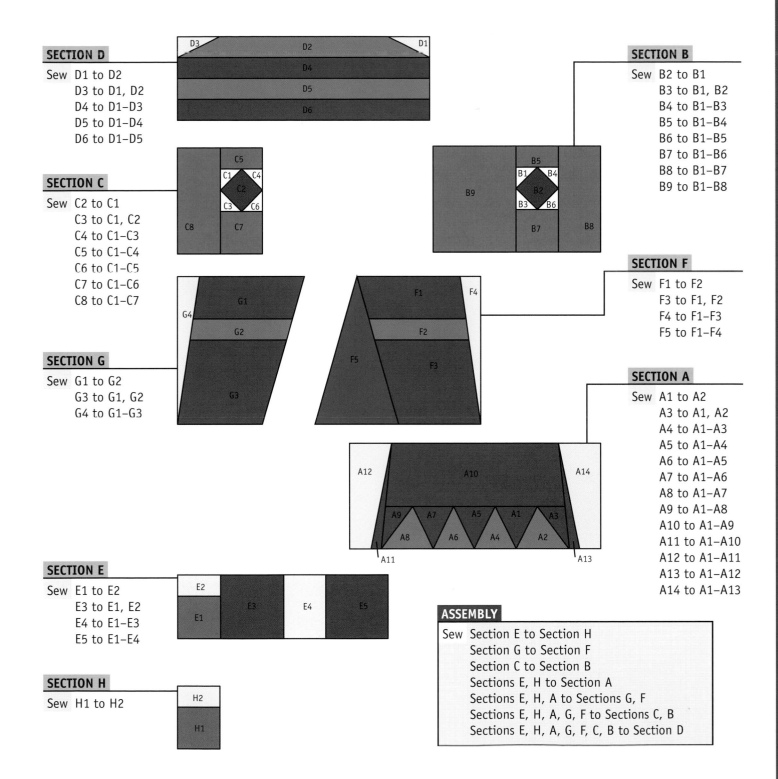

SECTION D

Sew D1 to D2
    D3 to D1, D2
    D4 to D1–D3
    D5 to D1–D4
    D6 to D1–D5

SECTION C

Sew C2 to C1
    C3 to C1, C2
    C4 to C1–C3
    C5 to C1–C4
    C6 to C1–C5
    C7 to C1–C6
    C8 to C1–C7

SECTION G

Sew G1 to G2
    G3 to G1, G2
    G4 to G1–G3

SECTION E

Sew E1 to E2
    E3 to E1, E2
    E4 to E1–E3
    E5 to E1–E4

SECTION H

Sew H1 to H2

SECTION B

Sew B2 to B1
    B3 to B1, B2
    B4 to B1–B3
    B5 to B1–B4
    B6 to B1–B5
    B7 to B1–B6
    B8 to B1–B7
    B9 to B1–B8

SECTION F

Sew F1 to F2
    F3 to F1, F2
    F4 to F1–F3
    F5 to F1–F4

SECTION A

Sew A1 to A2
    A3 to A1, A2
    A4 to A1–A3
    A5 to A1–A4
    A6 to A1–A5
    A7 to A1–A6
    A8 to A1–A7
    A9 to A1–A8
    A10 to A1–A9
    A11 to A1–A10
    A12 to A1–A11
    A13 to A1–A12
    A14 to A1–A13

ASSEMBLY

Sew Section E to Section H
     Section G to Section F
     Section C to Section B
     Sections E, H to Section A
     Sections E, H, A to Sections G, F
     Sections E, H, A, G, F to Sections C, B
     Sections E, H, A, G, F, C, B to Section D

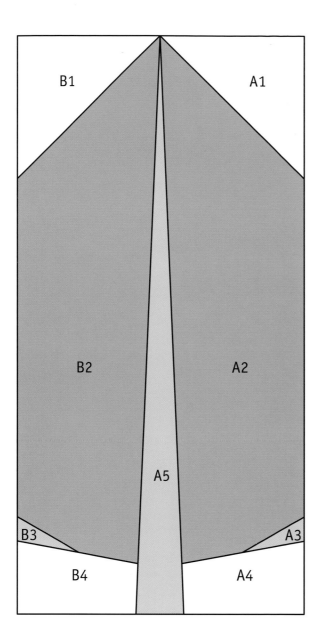

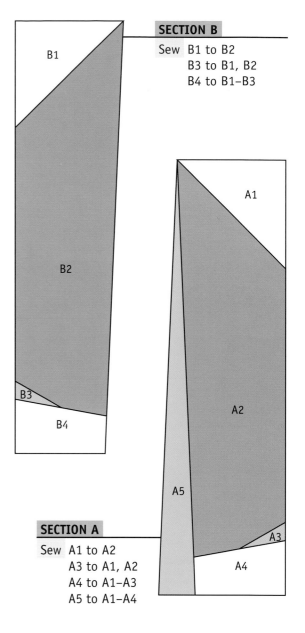

SECTION B

Sew B1 to B2
     B3 to B1, B2
     B4 to B1–B3

SECTION A

Sew A1 to A2
     A3 to A1, A2
     A4 to A1–A3
     A5 to A1–A4

ASSEMBLY

Sew Section A to Section B

See the block and story of Feather on page 58.

See the block and
story of Kokopelli
on page 60.

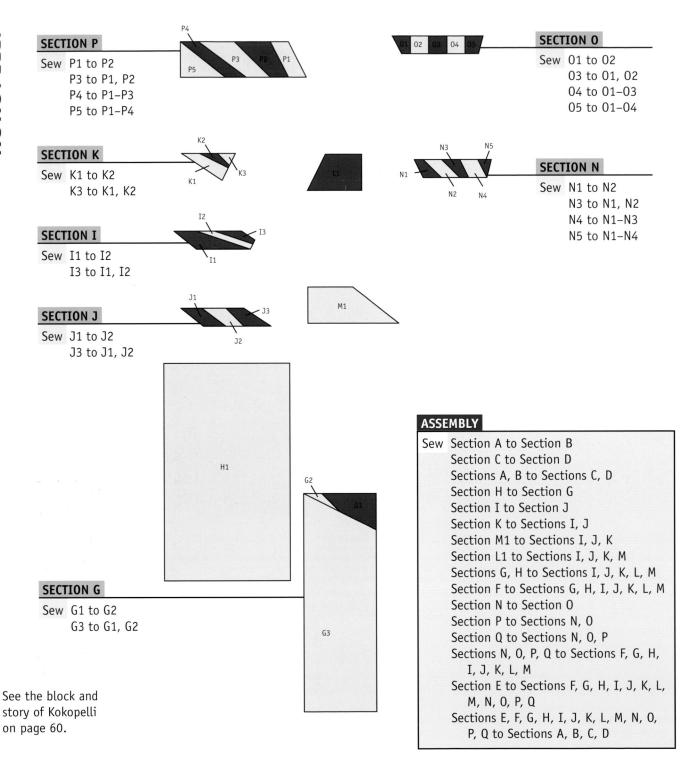

SECTION P

Sew P1 to P2
P3 to P1, P2
P4 to P1–P3
P5 to P1–P4

SECTION O

Sew O1 to O2
O3 to O1, O2
O4 to O1–O3
O5 to O1–O4

SECTION K

Sew K1 to K2
K3 to K1, K2

SECTION N

Sew N1 to N2
N3 to N1, N2
N4 to N1–N3
N5 to N1–N4

SECTION I

Sew I1 to I2
I3 to I1, I2

SECTION J

Sew J1 to J2
J3 to J1, J2

SECTION G

Sew G1 to G2
G3 to G1, G2

See the block and
story of Kokopelli
on page 60.

ASSEMBLY

Sew Section A to Section B
Section C to Section D
Sections A, B to Sections C, D
Section H to Section G
Section I to Section J
Section K to Sections I, J
Section M1 to Sections I, J, K
Section L1 to Sections I, J, K, M
Sections G, H to Sections I, J, K, L, M
Section F to Sections G, H, I, J, K, L, M
Section N to Section O
Section P to Sections N, O
Section Q to Sections N, O, P
Sections N, O, P, Q to Sections F, G, H,
I, J, K, L, M
Section E to Sections F, G, H, I, J, K, L,
M, N, O, P, Q
Sections E, F, G, H, I, J, K, L, M, N, O,
P, Q to Sections A, B, C, D

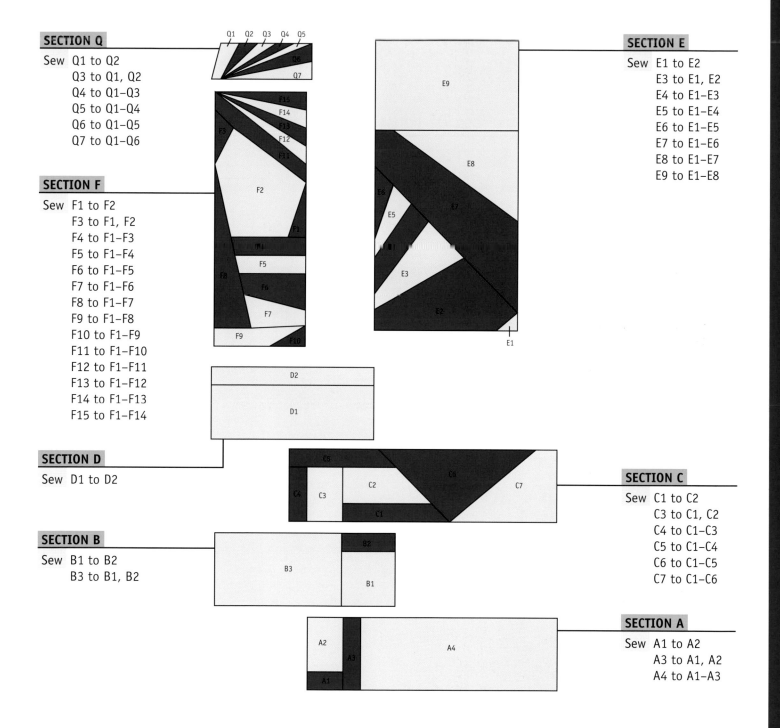

SECTION Q

Sew Q1 to Q2
     Q3 to Q1, Q2
     Q4 to Q1–Q3
     Q5 to Q1–Q4
     Q6 to Q1–Q5
     Q7 to Q1–Q6

SECTION F

Sew F1 to F2
     F3 to F1, F2
     F4 to F1–F3
     F5 to F1–F4
     F6 to F1–F5
     F7 to F1–F6
     F8 to F1–F7
     F9 to F1–F8
     F10 to F1–F9
     F11 to F1–F10
     F12 to F1–F11
     F13 to F1–F12
     F14 to F1–F13
     F15 to F1–F14

SECTION D

Sew D1 to D2

SECTION B

Sew B1 to B2
     B3 to B1, B2

SECTION E

Sew E1 to E2
     E3 to E1, E2
     E4 to E1–E3
     E5 to E1–E4
     E6 to E1–E5
     E7 to E1–E6
     E8 to E1–E7
     E9 to E1–E8

SECTION C

Sew C1 to C2
     C3 to C1, C2
     C4 to C1–C3
     C5 to C1–C4
     C6 to C1–C5
     C7 to C1–C6

SECTION A

Sew A1 to A2
     A3 to A1, A2
     A4 to A1–A3

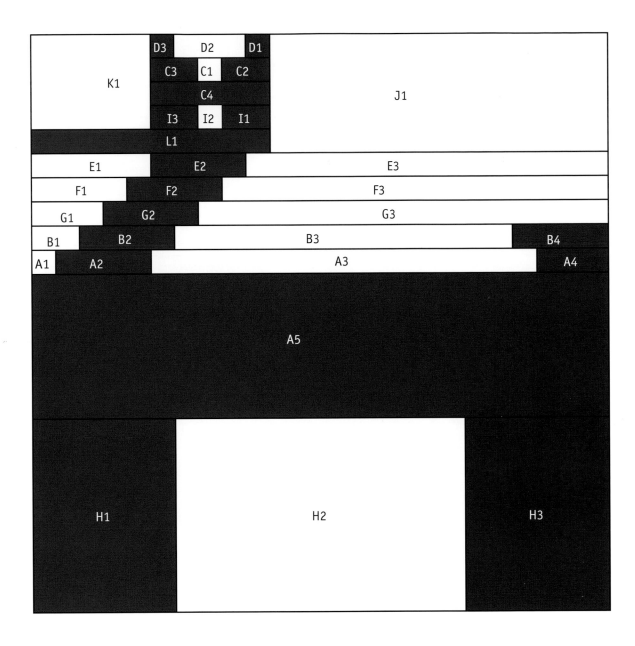

See the block and
story of Llama
on page 66.

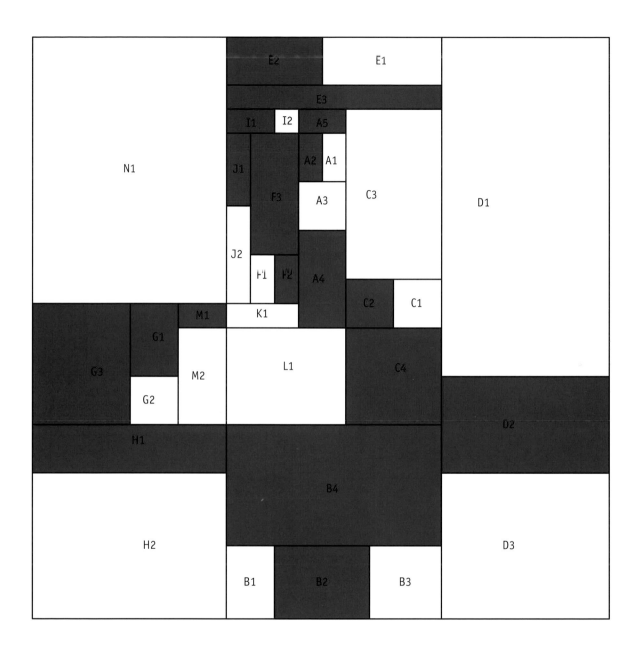

See the block and story of Nanuma Duck on page 68.

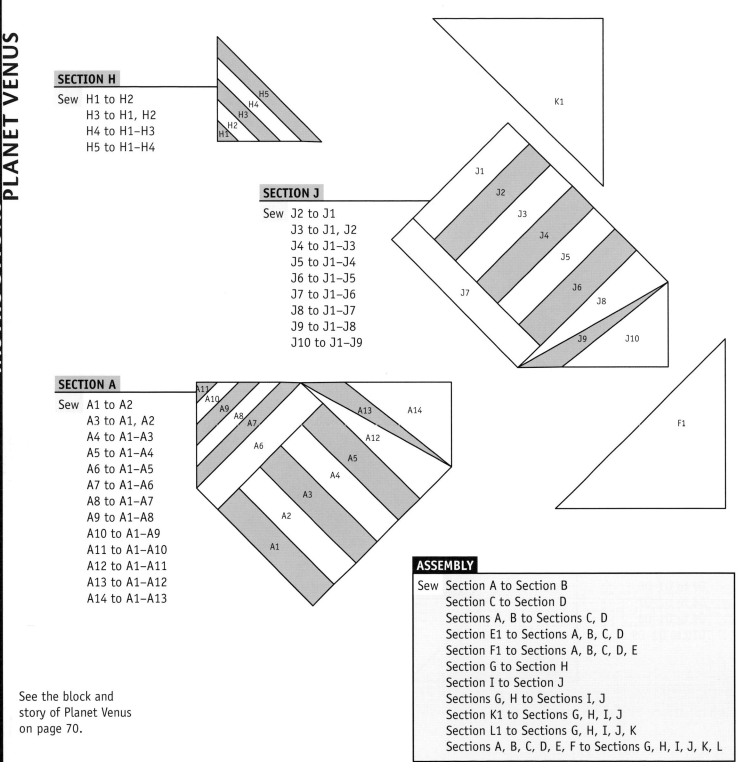

SECTION H

Sew H1 to H2
H3 to H1, H2
H4 to H1–H3
H5 to H1–H4

SECTION J

Sew J2 to J1
J3 to J1, J2
J4 to J1–J3
J5 to J1–J4
J6 to J1–J5
J7 to J1–J6
J8 to J1–J7
J9 to J1–J8
J10 to J1–J9

SECTION A

Sew A1 to A2
A3 to A1, A2
A4 to A1–A3
A5 to A1–A4
A6 to A1–A5
A7 to A1–A6
A8 to A1–A7
A9 to A1–A8
A10 to A1–A9
A11 to A1–A10
A12 to A1–A11
A13 to A1–A12
A14 to A1–A13

See the block and
story of Planet Venus
on page 70.

ASSEMBLY

Sew Section A to Section B
Section C to Section D
Sections A, B to Sections C, D
Section E1 to Sections A, B, C, D
Section F1 to Sections A, B, C, D, E
Section G to Section H
Section I to Section J
Sections G, H to Sections I, J
Section K1 to Sections G, H, I, J
Section L1 to Sections G, H, I, J, K
Sections A, B, C, D, E, F to Sections G, H, I, J, K, L

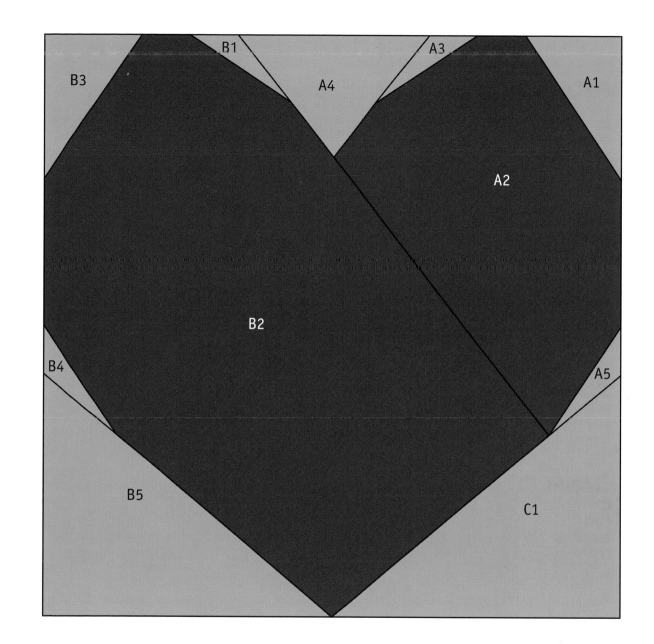

B1
A3
B3
A4
A1
A2
B2
B4
A5
B5
C1

See the block and
story of Heart on
page 76.

Index

FLEUR-DE-LYS

DUAFE

OM

Want even more? Find these exclusive bonus projects with photos, patterns, and step-by-step instructions at **www.larkbooks.com/crafts**.

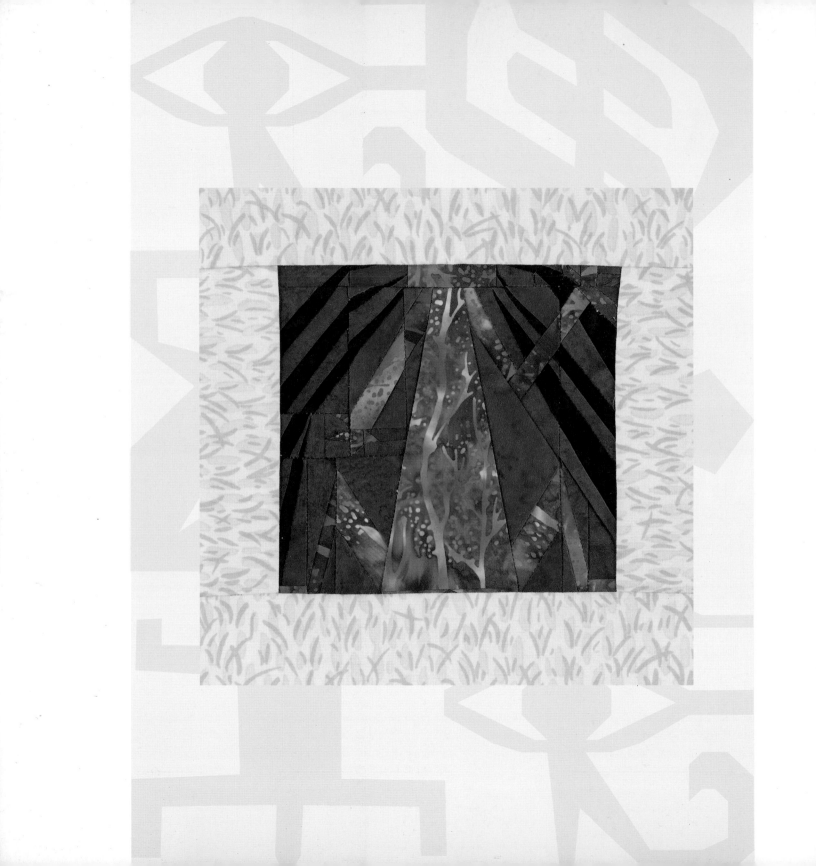